ISBN 978-1-332-14046-6
PIBN 10290102

This book is a reproduction of an important historical work. Forgotten Books uses state-of-the-art technology to digitally reconstruct the work, preserving the original format whilst repairing imperfections present in the aged copy. In rare cases, an imperfection in the original, such as a blemish or missing page, may be replicated in our edition. We do, however, repair the vast majority of imperfections successfully; any imperfections that remain are intentionally left to preserve the state of such historical works.

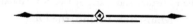

Similar Books Are Available from
www.forgottenbooks.com

HOME MANUFACTURE
OF FURS AND SKINS

MINK SKINS, CASED (RAW) AND DRESSED

HOME MANUFACTURE OF FURS AND SKINS

A Book of Practical Instructions Telling How to Tan, Dress, Color and Manufacture or Make into Articles of Ornament, Wear and Use

BY

ALBERT B. FARNHAM
Taxidermist and Furrier

PUBLISHED BY
A. R. HARDING
COLUMBUS, OHIO

CONTENTS

LIST OF ILLUSTRATIONS

ALBERT B. FARNHAM, Author

INTRODUCTION

Probably one of the oldest human industries is Home Dressing and Manufacturing of Furs and Skins, as this method of clothing the body has persisted from the stone age to the present time. As a happy combination of dress and ornament, furs will always continue to lead. At the present time the manufacture of furs has been highly developed, with the aid of machinery and specialized workmen it is conducted on a scale which compares favorably with any business activity.

However the principles remain the same, and good results can still be attained by hand labor. To the average "out-door" man it is a positive pleasure to see the stiff, dirty, raw skin develop into the soft, clean, flexible material, and later to shape it into a protection from the cold and an ornament combined.

In addition to the pleasure of tanning and making into some article for your home or office use, furs or skins caught or killed by yourself, there is a cash market for such articles. In fact, right here is the "Long End" of the profit. Raw fur skins that will bring, say $2.00 each in the raw, when tanned and made into some article, such as a muff, generally sell at several times the cost of the raw skin. The expense of manufacture is small and with lining added, is still but a trifle. During recent years many raw fur dealers have added tanning and manufacture of furs, skins, hides and pelts. Why? Because they realized that there was far more profit to sell as many skins as possible when manufactured. Can you blame them? Not in the least. At the same time why not reap some of the "Manufactured Furry" harvest yourself?

The demand for articles such as the average hunter, trapper, guide, farmer, rancher, etc., can make is ever increasing, and perhaps is an opportunity to make money at a business you enjoy. The tanning, dressing and making into muffs, scarfs, capes, caps, rugs, robes, etc., if fur skins or into gloves, moccasins, shirts, etc., if deer, woodchuck or sheep skins, can be done during slack time or bad weather.

In hundreds of places, not only cities, towns and villages but the country as well, there is a golden opportunity to build up a profitable business in articles manufactured from fur, pelts and hides. If your neighbors know that you are engaged in the business (and they will) it will soon be known for miles around, so that you will have calls and should make numerous sales. If you don't sell your output in this way, take samples and visit the various towns near you occasionally.

This is the day of the automobile and nearly all owners want fur robes. As a rule, these need not be made up of high priced skins, as warmth and comfort are usually what is most wanted. If you are in the coyote country these can generally be bought quite cheap—that is, if you are not a trapper. Even then, it may be cheaper to buy than to try to catch your supply. Cheap coon can also be worked up into robes. Coats can be made of furs from the cheapest to the more expensive—depends upon your trade. As a rule, cheap or moderate priced articles sell best. Rugs are also good sellers in some localities and are made in various styles, both from fur pelts and skins. Sheep skins are often used, but pelts with a certain length of wool must be selected for best results. Of the fur-bearers, those from bear down to the smallest size fox are used for rugs. Both coats and robes are now much used made from Galloway cattle hides.

Furs, pelts and hides are now used in practically every home to some extent. Why not make up some of your catch—either the poorest or best specimens—whichever you wish. In this connection let us ask a few questions:

Why pay a tanner big prices to do your tanning?

Why pay a cutter big prices to do your fur or hide cutting?

Why pay big prices for lining—satin, brocade—when you can buy it cheaper?

Why pay big prices for felt lining when you can buy it cheap?

Why pay a retailer of furs robes, etc., a big profit on top of what the tanner, cutter and manufacturer charges him when you can get *all* these profits yourself?

Albert B. Farnham

HOME MANUFACTURE OF FURS AND SKINS

CHAPTER I.

SOME FACTS AND GENERAL PRINCIPLES FOR FUR AND SKIN WORKERS.

IN the raw state, animal skins are roughly separated in three classes as follows:

1st. Horse, Cow, Ox, adult animals—Hides.

2nd. Horse, Cow, Ox, young or yearling animals—Kips.

3rd. Young Calf, Sheep, Goat, Deer, and smaller varieties—Skins.

It is with the latter class that we have principally to deal, though a few well haired specimens of the first two are used for coats and robes, by far the larger number are dehaired and converted into leather.

To understand the nature of the change worked by tanning in the animal hide it is necessary to refer briefly to its structure. It consists of three layers, the epidermis, derma and a fatty under tissue. Of these the epidermis itself has practically two coats, (a) the outer horny surface, and (b) a watery cellular one connecting it with the underlying derma. The outer coating is being shed and renewed continually from the cellular coat beneath. The derma or corin, is

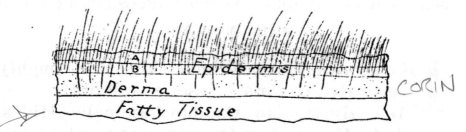

CORIN

SECTION OF SKIN OR HIDE, (MAGNIFIED)

the true skin, and leather making tissue. The inner layer of fatty tissue between the derma and the flesh and fat contains the perspiratory and sebaceous glands.

The moist animal skin undergoes decomposition very rapidly, if dried becomes stiff and heavy, or if boiled with water is changed into soluble glue. The object of tanning is to bring the skin into such a condition that decay is arrested, and after drying it no longer forms a stiff, horny mass but an opaque tissue, insoluble in water, fibrous and pliable. When dressed as furs such skins should retain the complete epidermis with its accompanying hair or fur.

The best authorities believe that tanning is more a physical than chemical process, and that the function of the tanning material is chiefly to penetrate the pores of the skin and envelope the individual fibres so that in drying they are prevented from adhering and so stiffening the whole mass.

In making true leather, both the epidermis and the under tissue are removed leaving the derma alone. This is composed of interlacing fibres, between which is found an albuminoid substance called coriin. This is insoluble in water alone but soluble in lime water and so removed in large part by the process of liming when making regular leather.

Though sometimes tanned hides are used for making rugs, the many processes of preparing skins for furriers use are usually quite distinct from ordinary leather making. The process of preserving skins in a condition for use as leather or garments, broadly spoken of as Tanning, may be separated into four quite different branches.

I.

VEGETABLE TANNING.

Using tannic acid derived from barks, leaves and vegetable gums. Nearly all heavy leather is so treated.

II.

MINERAL TANNING, SOMETIMES CALLED TAWING

This is done by the use of mineral salts, and

is pre-eminently the fur dresser's method, though dressers prepare some heavy skins by combination tanning, adding Gum Catechu or Terra Japonica to the alum or acid formula.

III.

OIL TANNING.

As buckskin and chamois are treated, removing the uncombined oil from the skins by pressure and chemical action and replacing it with other preparations.

IV.

COMBINATION TANNING.

Using both tannic acid and mineral salts combined, chiefly for leather and more rapid than a strictly vegetable process. The well known chrome leather, so durable for shoes, is made by one of the combination processes.

Making use of the term in its general sense, we refer to fur dressing as tanning, though to be strictly technical, tawing would be the proper term to use. The preparation called Mineral Tanning, Tawing or White Leather Dressing, is carried on in many forms, but all the methods consist practically of three distinct operations: 1, Fleshing; 2, Tawing or Preserving the skins, and the 3rd, Currying or softening them.

Fleshing consists in removing every particle of fat and flesh still remaining on the skin, and also the inner skin, which locks up and protects to a great extent the true skin from both mechanical and chemical action.

In tawing, the skins are immersed in some liquid preservative, being occasionally stirred about so that all parts of them are operated on equally. They are weighted down so as to be quite covered and left in this liquid for varying lengths of time, depending somewhat on the temperature and the thickness of the skins. When the action of the preservative is complete, it may be determined by pinching or cutting the skin of the back of the neck, the thickest part of the skin. The tawing completed the skins are removed, stretched to their full extent and allowed to become partly dry.

Currying proper, consists in stretching, separating and softening the fibres of the skin by some chemical means, such as working with a blunt edged knife or other tool, stretching, rolling, rubbing and pulling with the hands, etc. The above is about the general procedure, though amended and modified to suit the material and individual.

For instance, thin and delicate skins are often tawed before fleshing at all. Skins thus treated, and tawed in a solution (of alum and salt for instance) are converted into a substance resembling leather though different from it. There has been no chemical combination, however, analagous to that formed by the gelatine and tannic acid in ordinary tanning as the gelatine, alum and salt, can be again separated by treatment with water. Dressing the tawed skin with a paste of yolk of egg, flour and water or other oily pastes tend to resist this deleterious effect of water and keep the skins soft and pliable.

Alum was probably first used in tawing skins and is still used, though on account of its action in plumping or thickening the skin it has been to a great extent superceded by various acids. These, if properly used, destroy the glue in the skin so that currying leaves it porous and soft, a layer of inert fibres in which the hair or fur is securely rooted.

In skin dressers parlance the acid "kills the rubber" in the skin. Of course if a very strong acid solution is allowed to remain in the skin after disposing of the gelatine, the fibres themselves will be attacked and destroyed. Hence the necessity of thoroughly washing out, or scouring. Clear water will remove the salt or alum but acid tawed skins should be scoured with an alkali solution which will tend to neutralize any remaining acid. Dirty and greasy skins are treat-

ed with benzine baths and hot absorbents to clean
the fur, as no matter how well a skin may be
dressed otherwise, matted and dirty fur is not
wanted by civilized people.

Tanning and skin garment
making is one of the oldest
human industries, as long before men dreamed of textile fabrics, they were clothing themselves in the skins of the animals they ate. The gap 'between
the lady on the avenue and the
cave woman is not as long as it
seems. From the days when
stone age tools were fleshing
skins or when Simon the tanner
dwelt by the sea (a good supply
of salt water) on down to the
present electrical age, the element of hand labor
enters largely into fur and skin working.

STONE SKIN
DRESSING TOOL.
(Collected by A. B.
Farnham)

The industry has become highly specialized
in all the large cities of the world where it is
carried on with trained operatives and expensive
machinery, still there seems to be a place for the
hand worker who can combine a working knowledge of the necessary processes with such manual
dexterity and neatness as will insure a durable
and well finished article, useful and ornamental
alike.

In the small towns and country neighborhoods there is often difficulty to get a few fur articles made up from the raw skins. The expense of transportation and delay of sending such work to some large establishment give the local worker considerable advantage.

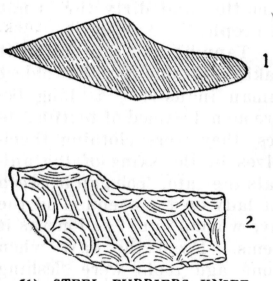

(1) STEEL FURRIERS KNIFE
(2) STONE KNIFE

Before proceeding further it might be well to give some attention to what a large dealer in raw furs and skins published some years ago as a caution to the inexperienced. He says thousands of dollars worth of valuable hides and skins are ruined each year by trappers and farmers trying to tan fur skins. Many of the quick tanning processes are not what they are claimed to be—there being no stretch to the hide when tanned and no furrier will buy them.

Should the beginner have the correct formula, he seldom does a good job, as it takes a lot of experience, and for heavy hides for robes, etc., special machinery to scrape or split them down thin. It is all very well for people to be energetic and try, but they ought to experiment on skins of no market value, such as woodchuck, squirrel, belgian hare and pig skins. When they succeed well on these, try dog cat, etc., before trying the more valuable ones.

This is good advice as anyone can see, but there is no reason why the energetic and persevering beginner cannot master the principles of fur dressing and working. The great difference between the price of the raw material and the finished product is attractive, but it should be borne in mind that there is usually a good reason for it.

Beginning with the trapper, he receives cash for his catch usually and that investment is tied up until the finished fur is delivered to the wearer (and sometimes for months afterward). Very few furs in the regular trade are worn the same season as taken, more often two years or more elapse with interest charges going on and the expense of the various handlings being added from time to time.

Tanning comes first, and here you say there is some graft for a tanned skin costs more than a raw one, plus the tanning charge. This is accounted for by the fact that many apparently sound skins will show up damaged or even be a total loss after dressing. Hidden folds will slough, and improperly cured skins and those left too long in the grease will drop to pieces. They are dressed at "owner's risk" of damage so such loss is added to the value of the survivors. Thin and faded skins go to the dyer, and this work must be paid for before the furrier proper puts a knife to the skins.

The late winter and early spring is the slack time in the fur shops. The manufacturers are endeavoring to collect on the past season's sales, ascertain what remains unsold, and having skins tanned and dyed for another season. In the sweltering days of July and August the fur operators are figuratively and literally "up to their chins in work" and "making the fur fly." They, like the trapper, need their pay at the week or month end and no one will begrudge it to them, so it is added also to the burden already carried. By the time the wages of wholesale and retail salespeople, display fixtures, insurance and other necessary charges are added the result is formidable.

The raw skin worth at the start $1.00 must now bring from $2.00 to $4.00 or see a loss inflicted on some one who has helped in its progress to the finished article. It is estimated that omitting the manufacturers of traps, guns, boats and other equipment there are in the United States alone over 25,000 persons employed in the

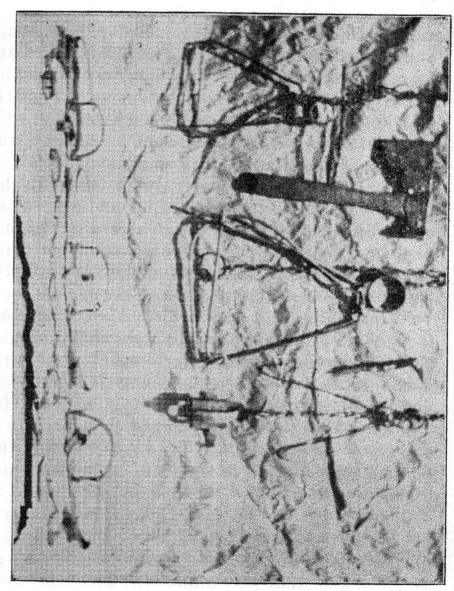

SIX SIZES AND PATTERNS STEEL TRAPS, HATCHET, KNIFE AND HOOKS
The Author has Caught More than One Grey Fox in the Larger Size Wire Trap

27

various branches of the fur trade. The average annual production of North America is estimated by a good authority to be 24,000,000 skins of all varieties, and the same person gives the yearly production of the world as having a value of $95,680,000 exclusive of skins used by natives and hunters for their own requirements.

New York City is the great fur center in this country for dressing, dyeing and manufacturing as well as accumulating the raw furs. St. Louis probably receives more shipments direct from trappers than any American market, and was the first city to hold auction sales similar to those held in London, England. New York leads as a consumer of finished furs, the sales to individuals there exceeding those in any other city of the world. London and Leipsic have claimed pre-eminence in dressing and dyeing but our fur workers are equal to any, and after two years of the great European War it was seen that this country was forging to the front in the fur trade of the world.

In your home manufacture of furs you will try to combine the work of many individuals in one in order that the profit may be greater; remember also that you alone will have the work to deal with in all its unpleasant phases, the hard and dirty task of the tanner, the tedious seams of the sewer and skin cutters puzzles will be yours, with perhaps salesmen's and collector's duties added, for good measure.

We all believe in the day of small things and in the fur business as in other lines of endeavor some of the greatest successes have resulted from the smallest beginnings. Ever since about 1870 there has been a steady rush of people to get a share of a trade which they evidently believed still yielded as large a profit as was secured by the traders who two centuries ago swapped beads and jack-knives for skins with the unsophisticated savages. Many to their sorrow soon discovered that if honestly conducted, the fur business like any other pays the dealer only a fair margin.

The responsibility of the dealer when purchasing furs must be apparent to all who remember what a large trade is carried on in what may be termed artificial products. The common and cheaper furs are now often so prepared as to resemble rarer and costlier articles. The skill with which piecing is done is somewhat marvelous. All clippings and cuttings of furs have their uses and pass into different hands for various purposes. The life of a fur also depends largely upon the method of dressing and the quality of the dye used in coloring.

The average purchaser cannot possibly have the knowledge that will protect him from being

imposed upon by unscrupulous dealers. There
are, however, so many responsible furriers and
fur dealers, large and small, that no one except
those who are looking for "something for nothing" need be the victim of fraud or deception.

The story of the furriers is not so full of
dramatic interest as the history of the Fur Traders and Trappers, but they are the "men behind
the guns" without whose prosaic efforts to make
furs fashionable, and to stimulate the demand at
various times for different species by the creaticn
of new styles, peltries never could have become
valuable enough to cause the traders and trappers to leave their homes and risk their lives in
the pursuit of their calling.

CHAPTER II.

CORRECT MODES OF SKINNING FUR ANIMALS.

THE professional fur worker has usually but little need of the information in this and the following two chapters, as nearly all the skins received by him are dry or cured. The home tanner, however, gets much of his work in the green state, often indeed receiving the entire animal, the skin of which is to be removed and prepared for use.

By following a few simple directions almost any one can do this so that the skin will be in good condition for either transportation, or storage in the dry undressed state or immediate dressing. Many people seem to imagine there is some mystery in the skinning process, and rather than undertake it will often ship an entire animal long distances. Not only does this add to the expense, but by being left on the carcass so long many fur skins are spoiled entirely or at least damaged.

As an example we once received in Washington, D. C., a black bear, shipped by a sportsman in the Adirondacks, who desired a rug made of the skin. It had been headed up in a tight barrel and expressed to a friend who was out of town for the week end at the time, and as this was in the early fall the effect when the barrel was opened can be better imagined than described. Needless to say the skin was useless and the express charges of $2.00 or so wasted. A couple of hours work on the part of sportsman or guide would have saved a good trophy and reduced the expense of shipping to fifty cents or so.

The main idea is to get the skin off entire and with as few accidental cuts as possible. If the entire skin is removed it is a simple matter to put it in shape even if badly cut or if the opening cuts are made in undesirable places, while if parts of it are cut away it becomes very difficult to repair properly.

The proper mode of skinning varies somewhat according to the use contemplated for the dressed furs. Many hunters and trappers do not realize that there is a very practical reason for "cased" or "open" skinning and "square" or "long" handling of various skins. A moment's thought will show that the nearer the raw fur can be made to approximate the finished article in shape, the less work is imposed on the furrier, the less material will be wasted in shaping, and more valuable such skins will be.

Muskrats are usually "cased," as the shorter furred bellies are often made up separate from the backs. If they were skinned "open" it would be necessary to fit together and sew a seam the entire length of the skin to use them so. For all

"CASED" AND "OPEN" STRETCHED RACCOON SKINS

small animals a good sharp pocket knife will be sufficient and for those of larger size a common butcher or hunting knife. Gambrel hooks of some kind render the skinning process easier and may be either purchased or made as follows:

SKINNING OPOSSUM
(CASED)

Get a piece of heavy wire, about No. 8 size, 18 inches long, bend it in the middle something like a ∧ shape, turn up each end for an inch or so in a hook, and tie one end of a foot of stout cord to the middle. If a small wire hook is fastened to the other end of this cord it can be thrown over a branch or nail and the animal suspended by inserting the hooks under the heel tendons after starting cuts down the hind legs.

This enables the operator to use both hands and the cord permits turning the animal from side to side as needed during the process. This arrangement will handle anything not larger than a fox. Large animals, skinned "open" are laid on the back and turned from side to side, or a wooden gambrel and piece of rope used to suspend them.

To remove a skin "cased" lay the animal on its back and inserting the knife point under the skin of each hind foot, slit down the back of the legs to the base of the tail, slit the tail its full length on the under side, and slit up the back of the front legs of such skins as mink, marten, fisher and fox.

Animals like these that have the feet furred, may have the skin of the feet, nails and all removed, by pulling the skin down and severing each toe at the point above the nail; if the feet are not furred, pass the knife around the ankles and peel the skin down the hind legs until the body is reached. The scent glands are to be cut around carefully and the tail skinned out.

In many cases the tail may be quickly stripped without slitting, but preservatives are not so easily applied and often the tail sheath will stick together and eventually slip part of the fur when so stripped. Tails of muskrat, beaver and opossum are worthless on furs and may be chopped off where the fur ends before skinning.

The skin is pulled down over the head, wrong side out like a sock, using the knife to cut any ligaments attaching it to the flesh; directing the blade towards the body rather than the skin that no cuts be made in it. Bits of flesh and fat adhering are most safely removed afterwards. The fore legs reached, they are drawn back out of the skin which is severed at the ankles or toes as the case may require.

The ears are next reached and cut off not too close to the skull, the membrane at the eyes cut through and the lips reached. Don't get impatient when so nearly done and slash off the skin of nose and chin but cut carefully a moment leaving the lips and bare nose on the skin, they will dry without splitting from the inside unless the animal is a large one and the weather warm. The carcass of a well skinned animal will have no tufts of fur adhering to it.

In skinning "open" an additional cut is made from the chin to the tail and the front legs are slit down to it generally, though in the case of the raccoon the front legs are not slit all their length and the beaver is only cut from chin to tail, the legs not slit at all so it stretches in an oval shape.

Large animals such as the bear, puma, or mountain lion, jaguar, leopard and tiger, the skins of which are mostly used as rugs should always be skinned "open," with claws attached to the feet and heads entire. Do not throw away the skulls of any such animals received in the flesh but clean them and preserve the teeth for use in mounting the heads.

The quickest way to do this is to drop the skinned head into an old pot or tin of water and

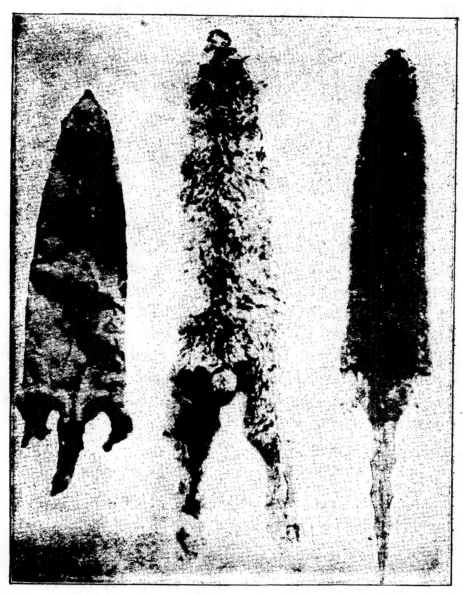

SOME "CASED" STRETCHED RAW SKINS — HOUSE CAT, LYNX, OTTER.

boil it until the flesh begins to get tender. Watch it, as if boiled too long the bones will separate at the little dove-tailed joints of the skull, called sutures, the teeth drop out and render it worthless. While warm the flesh is cut and scraped away, the hole at the back of the skull enlarged with a chisel or hatchet and the brain scooped out.

Hang up to dry out, when it can be attached entire to the skin by a cord or wire, or the teeth plates only sawed off and preserved. If not wanted for mounting such teeth are readily sold to the makers of artificial papier mache heads, bringing from 15 or 20 cents per set for a fox, to $1.00 or $2.00 for the larger animals. Some skin dealers buy them, but the best prices will be had from taxidermists and manufacturing furriers.

SKIN "CASED".

Weasel, Fisher, Muskrat Otter, Mink, Fox, Civet, Wild Cat, House Cat, Marten, Opossum, Skunk, Lynx.

SKIN "OPEN".

Raccoon, Wolverine, Beaver, Bear, Wolf, Puma, Badger, Coyote.

A few moleskins have been collected for furs in this country from time to time. They should

WELL HANDLED CANADIAN RED FOX SKINS

These pelts were from foxes caught, skinned and stretched by the trapper who had them and himself photographed before selling.

(Photo and description from Fur Buyers' Guide—See page 286.)

be handled "square" like raccoon to work up to the best advantage. Especially the skins of coyote and raccoon are often "cased" for use as ladies' furs, but for the great majority "open" square handling is best.

After skinning and before stretching, if the fur is wet it should be dried, and burrs, mud and bloodclots removed from it. Clear water and a rag, sponge, or brush will remove the blood and mud can be beaten and brushed out when dry. To dry wet fur, take the skin by first one end and then the other and whirl it rapidly round in the air.

If to be dressed immediately the skin may be salted raw or in some cases placed in the tanning solution or pickle. For shipping, storing or sale as raw fur, stretching and curing or drying is the next step after removing any considerable lumps of flesh, fat or muscle from the inside of the skin.

Fatty hides like the bear, skunk, raccoon and opossum may be so thickly coated as to require the use of a fleshing knife on a beam, but the skinning knife and thumb and finger are sufficient for fleshing such as muskrat, mink and marten. Before using the flesher on the beam, remove all burrs and lumps of mud from the fur or a hole will be cut in the skin at each one in the operation.

CHAPTER III.

CASED skins are dried on rather long and narrow stretchers which may be either skeleton frames of wood or metal or one or several pieces of wood. One form which is widely sold consists of two curved pieces of flat steel hinged together at the nose and adjustable by opening or closing at the rear. A non-adjustable stretcher for small skins such as muskrat, is often made of a 48 inch piece of heavy galvanized wire, bent into shape and the ends twisted together with plyers.

I am not partial to metal stretchers of any kind and they should never be used at all unless thoroughly galvanized or rust will damage the skins. We once received two skins in apparent good order, to be dressed for rugs, which had been so rusted that a narrow strip from head to tail on each side dropped to pieces completely.

For skeleton wood stretchers use straight osier, willow or hickory switches as thick as the finger. Cut two short cross pieces, and carefully bending the long piece at the middle nail these in with a small wire nail at each end. A handful

41

of shingle nails and a clump of osier sprouts will make a full outfit of "cased" stretchers when it is desirable to travel light.

A modification of this eliminates the need of tacks or nails even in stretching muskrats. The sapling cut for a stretcher is long enough to have a surplus of one or two feet which is left on the butt end. The small end is bent into the proper shape for the stretcher, crosspiece and all and twisted or lashed in place with bark.

In skinning the muskrat, the tail is split on each side and skinned off as two strips connected with the under and upper side of the pelt. After drawing on the stretcher these strips are pulled back and tied around the crosspiece. The skin of the hind legs is drawn back and the knife blade forced through it and into the wood a short distance at a slant. When the knife is withdrawn the edge of the skin will catch in the cut and hold it securely.

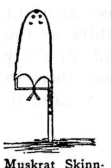

Muskrat Skinned and Stretched—"Tied with His Own Tail."

By pushing the long end of the sapling stretcher into the ground it will hold it upright to dry. For ingenuity in making the materials at hand serve the purpose this seems hard to beat. When the skin is dry the switch is bent or broken and removed. Absolutely nothing but a knife and switch are required to skin and stretch a muskrat when "tied with his own tail." Natural forked branches are sometimes made use of, but on account of their poor shape and variations, hardly any two being alike, they are not recommended as fur stretchers.

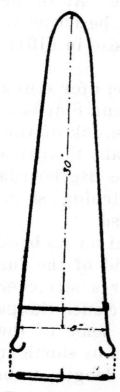

Heavy Galvanized Wire Skunk Skin Stretcher.

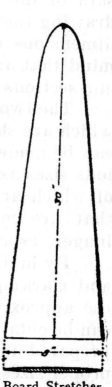

Board Stretcher for Skunk.

For making board stretchers soft pine, poplar, cedar or other light material is best, and old dry goods boxes are often taken apart and used. Board stretchers should be planed and the edges smoothly chamfered and rounded. The three piece or wedge stretcher is made by ripping a wedge shaped piece from the center after the outline of the board has been finished. For convenience and to prevent buckling when inserted in the skin, nail two small cleats to the base of one side piece.

A thin board stretcher in one piece with a narrow "sword stick" on each side will fully stretch and cure the skin faster and better than where only the outside is exposed to the air. When fully dry removing the swords relieves the skin of the stretching equally as well as withdrawing the wedge of the other style. As to the dimensions of these boards it must be borne in mind that animals vary greatly in size in different sections of the country.

The two illustrations of stretchers for skunk which are shown as 30 inches long and 8 at base can be made larger or smaller for skunk of various sizes as well as for other animals, the skins of which are handled cased. Some use boards that are more pointed thus stretching skins longer, especially the head and nose.

By laving the unskinned animal on its back and marking around it near the end of the fur the approximate size and shape for a stretcher can be obtained, but it is well to have such things prepared in advance, so will give some of the proper sizes. The measurement given as shoulder is usually about $\frac{1}{3}$ or $\frac{1}{4}$ the entire length, from the nose.

Muskrat, (dimensions in inches). Length 20 to 24. Base 5 to 7. Shoulder 4 to $6\frac{1}{4}$.

Mink, Marten. Length 18 to 28. Base $2\frac{1}{2}$ to $4\frac{3}{4}$. Shoulder 2 to $4\frac{1}{4}$.

Weasel. Length 16. Base 2 to 2½. Shoulder 1¼ to 2.

Opossum, Skunk. Length 25 to 30. Base 6 to 8. Shoulder 5 to 6¼.

Raccoon. Length 28 to 3⁰ Base 8½ to 10¼. Shoulder 6½ to 8½.

Fox, Fisher. Length 42 to 45. Base 6½ to 8. Shoulder 5 to 6.

Otter. Extra long so tail can be tacked out. Length 48 to 72. Base 6 to 8¼. Shoulder 5 to 6¼.

Lynx, Coyotes. Length 60 to 66. Base 11. Shoulder 7 to 9.

Animals the size of raccoon and larger require boards ½ to ¾ inches thick, for smaller ones ¼ inch thickness is sufficient.

These stretchers are inserted in the skins as they are removed, with fur side in, back on one side of the board, belly on the other, the skin is drawn on snugly and tacked at the hind feet, then the wedge or "swords" as the case may be are pushed in until it is fully stretched sideways, when a few more tacks across the base will secure it.

Skunk should have the tail spread and secured with a few tacks, and the otter's tail requires spreading and tacking at short intervals its entire length.

The front legs of lynx and coyote may be par-
tiafly distended by pieces of thin board like lath
or by bent twigs.

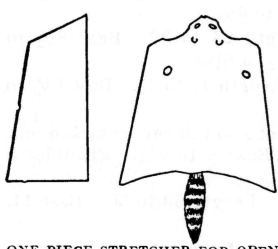

ONE PIECE STRETCHER FOR OPEN
RACCOON

Raccoon are
sometimes s k i n-
ned, c a s e d and
stretched o n a
board shaped like
the cut herewith.
The back of the
skin is placed on
the long *edge* of
this board, how-
ever, and when
dry it is c u t
down the front,
making an open skin of this shape. Many skins
are stretched open on the barn door, but the
method of lacing in a hoop or frame is far superior, as it allows the air access to both sides
and they are easily hung out of reach of dogs
or other animals. Bear and similar sizes require
rectangular frames well braced, while round or
oval hoops suit smaller skins.

These and the larger frames may be made in
the woods of saplings lashed together with cord
or wire. A sacking or sail needle with heavy
twine is used to lace the skins in place and the
lacing should be in four pieces, so that each side

can be loosened or stretched separately. Beaver are given an oval shape two or three inches longer than they are wide, raccoon nearly rectangular.

Use plenty of stitches or tacks to avoid drawing out in points. Stretching a "coon" skin with six nails does not enhance its value. Large tacks are easiest to handle and the brass headed upholstery variety suit for small skins, with wire shingle or box nails for large ones.

Never "peg out" skins if any other way to stretch is possible, as the necessary slits around the edge disfigure the skin and the dampness of the ground will hardly aid in drying, while exposed to both weather and animals. Many skins of polar bear are stretched thus for want of suitable material for drying frames in the Arctic where they are killed, and leopards and jaguars from the Tropics often receive the same treatment, though not for the same reason.

After a skin has been properly taken off and stretched it should be hung in some cool, dry, airy place until dry, before removing from the boards, with the exception that fox, marten and lynx are left two or three days until partially dried, then removed, turned fur side out and replaced. Do not cure furs in the sun or near a fire. Under a wagon shed, a bough house or a tent fly is a good place, or thick tree shade will do. Sometimes in camping it is necessary to

pack up and move before skins can be thoroughly
dried, and in such a case they may be exposed
to a little fire heat to dry the flesh sides so they
will not stick together.

If the weather is cool they will often keep
for some time without stretching or curing. We
once dressed a bunch of South American foxes,
(thirty days from the Straits of Magellan by
steamer), that had never been stretched or dried
and but little fur slipped.

Trappers usually skin their catch along the
trap line and carry the pelts turned fur out, so
leaves and dirt will not stick to them, to headquarters for stretching and curing.

The skin of a frozen animal is all right so
long as it remains frozen, but should be removed
when thawed out. Do not expose to intense heat
in the thawing process or the fur may be injured
before the flesh is thawed.

Much of this and the preceding chapters will
be unnecessary to many readers, as of late years,
handlers of fur skins have informed themselves
of the most up-to-date methods, still I have seen
a professional furrier stretch a green fox skin
on an inch board, hacked into a rough shape with
a hatchet.

When furs are thoroughly dry remove from
the boards string in loose bunches and hang in a
cool room, preferably a rather dark one, as too
much sunlight will fade most furs badly.

CHAPTER IV

HANDLING OTHER SKINS AND HIDES.

THOUGH intended for the dresser of skins, as the hides of all furbearers and other animals not larger than the deer are classified, it may be well to refer briefly to the handling of what are, strictly speaking, hides and of some smaller fur bearing skins also.

It is not our intention to direct how to turn heavy hides into leather, as to do so with any success or profit requires special and expensive apparatus, but only some points on their taking off and curing, before sending to a regularly equipped tannery.

The domestic animals liable to fall into our hands for skinning and curing are the horse, cattle, goat, sheep, pig, dog and cat. Remove the skins of all these except perhaps the cat, as directed in skinning animals open, making as few unnecessary cuts and jagged useless points and tags as you can. In the case of horned cattle split up the face and cut around the horns, remove all pieces of flesh and fat, spread out level on ground or floor and use plenty of coarse salt on the flesh side. If they are to be shipped green, heavy hides should remain thus for two days. **On** the third day turn over and salt well over the hair side, roll up flesh side out and ship in box or sack.

If desirable to dry the skin out to lighten transportation or to store it, after lying in the salt two or three days hang up over some poles until nearly dry, when it can be rolled or folded up with the hair side in. The skins of deer, moose and elk may be treated in the same way.

Don't leave hides lie around in a pile after skinning. To do so for an hour while the animal heat is in them may ruin them. Don't be stingy with salt, an extra five cents worth may save dollars and can hurt nothing.

In cool dry weather quite heavy hides may be cured without salt by simply drying, but would not advise trying it if salt is to be had. Keep them in the dry while curing, under a roof if you can.

The skins of goats, sheep, dogs and pigs may be laced in frames and cured without the use of salt quite readily. Dog skin, while not a very durable leather, can be used in many ways, and I have often wondered why it was not utilized to a greater extent in this country. Domestic cats receive treatment identical with their wild relatives.

There is quite a list of marine mammals an occasional skin of which may turn up, and more rarely the skin of some large fish. Among these are the seals, both fur and hair, sea lions, walrus, manatee, shark, ray, porpoise and even whale.

The seals and sea lions are usually skinned by making a single cut from chin to tail flippers along the under side and may be stretched and dried in a hoop, but are mostly salted without stretching. Most of the others on the list have another cut made down the back separating the skin in two sides which are salted without stretching.

The only species of whale the skin of which is utilized to any extent is the beluga or white whale, the skin of which is known as "porpoise leather," and is extremely adaptable for foot wear. The infrequent skins of fish to be dressed are salted to cure them also.

Frogs, lizards, snakes and most commonly alligators, represent the class of reptiles furnishing work for the skin dresser. Frogs and lizards are skinned open and salted, as the skins of all reptiles should be, in order to attain the best results in dressing. Snakes are split down the center of the under plates or scales from head to tail tip before skinning. Salt (with fine salt) if possible, if not, tack on a board in the shade until dry, then roll up.

ALLIGATOR SKINS — UNDER
SURFACE AND HORN BACK

In removing alligator skins two methods **are** followed, the most common being to cut the skin from the head to tail along each side of the horny ridge of the back. Cuts are made running from these longitudinal ones, to and along the middle of each of the legs on their outer sides. After cutting around the jaws the skin is peeled off in one piece. This is the usual method in the Gulf States where the horny back skin is not saved, at least from the larger specimens.

The skins from Mexico and Central America are opened by a cut, from lower jaw to tail in the middle of the under surface of the animal, with cuts along the inner sides of the legs from the wrists to the central line. This preserves the back entire, making the so-called "horn alligator" leather. Great care should be used in skinning, as knife cuts which are hardly noticeable in the raw skins become so apparent when dressed as to damage such skins greatly.

Immediately on removing, the inner surface of the skin should be carefully rubbed with fine salt, taking care to work it well into all folds and crevices. Fold the edges and skin of legs in, roll the skin up in a compact bundle and place in a cool, dry place. Never let the alligator hides dry out but after curing somewhat, salt again and pack in tight boxes or barrels, using plenty of salt.

Formerly only the skin from the underpart and sides of this animal were used, as the back is so heavily armored with horny plates that it was considered useless for leather except in the case of very small hides. Improvements in handling have made it possible to prepare the back almost as readily as the thinner parts, and the demand for such is mostly supplied by skins from Central America and Mexico, most of which have the back preserved entire. Skins from the United States are seldom cut "horn back" because they are not as flexible on the back as the Mexican variety.

The heads and paws are often left on small skins and mounted on the hand bags and satchels made of the leather. Large "gator" paws, dressed and furnished with clasps, make unique purses which find ready sale as souvenirs.

Hides over ten feet in length are seldom used owing to the hardness of the cuticular plates, making it difficult to so tan them as to have any value for purposes of leather, though some as long as seventeen feet have been prepared.

Bird skins are occasionally wanted dressed, usually the breasts of water fowl, such as grebes, ducks, loons and swans. The skin of the under part of the bodies of these birds is removed in one piece and stretched flat by tacking on a board. They are used for trimming hats and coats and sometimes for muffs and collarettes also. The Indians of the North sometimes make a raincoat of loon breasts. which sheds water very well.

CHAPTER V

STORING AND SHIPPING RAW FURS.

RAW furs should never be shipped in a green, uncured state even for short distances if it can be avoided. Unforseen occurrences may prevent delivery when expected and part or all of the shipment may be spoiled. If raw skins recently taken off are salted for two or three days and then rolled up with plenty of salt the chances will be better, but such packages need either a tight container or plenty of absorbents packed with them, as they are liable to drip moisture. The best plan is to stretch and dry all fur skins thoroughly. This not only prevents spoiling en route but greatly decreases the transportation charges.

Fatty skins should be well fleshed also; they are liable to be held in hot, close cars and warehouses, and the fat and grease, which must be removed anyway, will help to make the express charge higher. In packing furs, lay them flat with as little bending and folding as possible.

Skins with the fur side out should not be placed next the flesh side of others, but wrapped separately. Tie or bale all packages tightly with the coarser skins on the outside. Do not ship one cased skin inside another. Fold large skins with legs, head and fur inside.

Skunk skins that are scented may not be shipped by express or parcel post unless in a tight container. As this is hardly practicable or profitable, with a few skins at least, such skins should be de-odorized. To remove the odor of skunk from clothes or skins, soak them for thirty minutes to an hour in gasoline, wash well in it, wring out and hang in the open air until it evaporates. Don't do this near a lamp or fire of any kind and don't try to smoke while doing it. Outdoors is the best place to operate. If skins are scraped first, nearly all grease will be removed by this, but an additional process is necessary to clean the fur completely. Handlers of raw furs will do well to remember that a little gasoline will remove evil odors and grease from the hands at once.

When shipping raw skins by parcel post it is a good plan to wrap them in a piece of either old or new oilcloth before the final paper wrapping, as they will be thrown out of the mail if there is danger of the grease injuring other articles.

Express packages are best sewn up in burlap or cloth, even large bales of skins handling nicely with a double wrapping of burlap. All packages

OTTER CANADA   RED FOX NORTHERN   SILVER FOX NORTHERN   CROSS FOX CANADIAN   LYNX NORTHERN

NORTHERN FURS—OTTER, FOX, LYNX

Note the color and heavy fur. Photo from "Fur Buyers' Guide," which explains value of raw furs.

should be marked plainly inside and out with address of shipper and consignee.

Unless skins are thoroughly cleaned and cured they are apt to suffer during a sea voyage, the moist, close atmosphere of a ship's hold being particularly favorable to the development of mold and mildew.

When shipping skins for dressing or sale on approval they should all bear some mark, for even where the honesty of all parties concerned is beyond question, some confusion and mistakes are almost certain to occur where similar skins are handled in large numbers. Furs sent on approval are generally sealed with a metal, (tin or lead), seal and seal press, a small duplicate of that used on box car doors. Paper tags with price or other marks are threaded on the wire or cord loop.

Skins for dressing must be marked otherwise, as the seals would be in the workman's way. Raw Skin Stamps, consisting of a mallet or hammer, the face of which contains steel pins arranged to form various letters, are used for this purpose by furriers and dressers. The skin is laid on a block of rubber or a pad of some kind and struck a blow with the stamp, perforating it in the design of the stamp. This perforation is usually at some certain spot, as the center of the back, between the ears or at the base of the

NORTHWESTERN FURS — WILD CAT, MINK, MARTEN, BEAVER, WEASEL, MUSKRAT, WOLF

(Photo from "Fur Buyer's Guide"—see page 286.)

tail, where it cannot well be cut away and does not injure the fur at all.

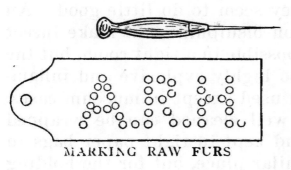

MARKING RAW FURS

An inexpensive marking apparatus is easily made for a few cents, and will answer all purposes where a small number of skins are to be handled. On a slip of sheet metal, tin, copper or brass, 1x3 inches, write or scratch your initials, and laying it on a wooden block with a hammer and awl prick the letters through. Smooth this on the back with a file and placing it on the skin to be marked, perforate through the holes in the marking plate with a sharp, slender awl. Additional letters or figures can be made to mark certain skins or lots of skins. Skins taken for dressing, if valuable, should be marked in the presence of customer or witnesses to avoid controversy.

To store raw furs over summer without cold storage is a risky proceeding in all except the Northern States, and one involving quite a little trouble. Probably the best way to keep any quantity would be to hang the skins, free from fat and flesh, in loose bunches in dry, cool and rather dark rooms.

Various moth deterents are used, such as naphthaline, tobacco, etc., but unless the room is about air tight they seem to do little good. An open dish of carbon bisulphide will make insect life absolutely impossible in a tight room, but the vapor from it is so highly explosive and inflammable it is seldom used except in museum cases.

A few skins well cleaned can be wrapped well separately and kept in tight paper bags in an airy loft or similar place, but for the holding over of any considerable amount of raw furs, storage at or about the freezing point is best. For such storage they may be tightly baled, reducing the charges to a minimum, as they are calculated on the cubic space occupied principally.

Cattle hides are frequently treated to prevent damage by insects during the summer by sprinkling them on both sides with a solution of arsenic made as follows:

Red or White Arsenic......10 lbs.
Concentrated Lye ....4 oz.
Water ....8 gals.

Put the arsenic and lye in a tub, pour the water over them and let stand a week. Mix one part of this with five parts of water and use in a garden sprinkler, or a sprayer would be more economical.

A shipper who packs his furs in good shape gives us these simple directions for baling so as to make a neat looking bundle substantial enough to arrive at its destination in good shape and look its best when opened.

Take a box with a bottom the size you wish the bottom of your bale of furs to be, and turn it bottom down on the floor near the wall. Then spread a piece of burlap on it large enough to hang over the edges a few inches all around. Put on this a piece of heavy paper a little smaller than the burlap. Now lay on your furs in a flat square pile the shape of the box. Brush the fur out straight and smooth as you place them in the pile. When all are in place cover with paper and burlap similar to that at the bottom.

Cover the top of the pile with several pieces of board crosswise of the bale. Nail a cleat to the wall somewhat below the top of the pile and catch one end of a scantling or heavy board under this cleat. This lever should come lengthwise of the bale and when well pressed down, get some one to hold it or fasten it, while you fold the edges of paper and burlap in neatly on both sides. With a sail needle and cord sew the burlap together along the sides, remove the lever, fold in and sew the ends and you have a trim, secure bundle. Put a stout cord around it lengthwise and crosswise a couple of times to furnish something to handle it by, tie the shipping tags on and the bale is ready for shipment.

CHAPTER VI.

INDIAN SKIN DRESSING.

WHILE the art of fur and skin dressing is at its greatest efficiency at the present time, probably the American Indian was at one time the best dresser of American animal skins, and the art of tanning as practiced now has been gradually evolved from primitive processes.

A writer says on this subject in regard to the European race: "The ancients detached the flesh from the skins with sharpened stones and dried them in the sun, after which they were rubbed with oil or grease extracted from the intestines of the slaughtered animals, and a polish was added to the skins by rubbing them with porous stones.

The hides of bullocks, horses and other large animals were used to make the tents which sheltered the early Patriarchs, and the skins of the leopards, tigers and smaller animals supplied the wearing apparel with which they were able to glorify themselves before their fellowmen.

At a later period the adhering particles of flesh remaining on the skin when it was wrenched from the animal were removed with bone, stone and iron instruments, and the skins were washed so as to open the pores and cleanse them from dust and dirt. After this was done they were exposed to the frost.

"Later still it was discovered that the skins would be greatly improved by plunging them into water containing a solution of alum, and then putting them into vinegar. These baths protected the skins from rotting. After they had been dried in the shade the skins were moistened again and beaten, stretched and otherwise manipulated until they were supple, clean, and free from disagreeable odors."

Probably the best description of Indian skin dressing was written by Catlin in 1832 while among the Crows and Sioux. Paintings made by him at that time, now in the National Museum, show squaws unhairing and dressing buffalo hides laced in a frame and pegged on the ground. The work is described as follows

"The Crows, like the Blackfeet, are beautifully costumed, and perhaps with somewhat more of taste and elegance; inasmuch as the skins of which their dresses are made are more delicately and whitely dressed. The art of dressing skins belongs to the Indians in all countries; and the Crows surpass the civilized world in the beauty of their skin-dressing. The art of tanning

GREAT COMANCHE VILLAGE, TEXAS, IN 1834.

Women dressing skins. No. 346, page 257.

(Plate 164, Vol. II, Catlin's Eight Years.)

is unknown to them, so far as civilized habits and arts have not been taught them; yet the art of dressing skins, so far as we have it in the civilized world, has been (like hundreds of other ornamental and useful customs which we are practicing) borrowed from the savage, without our ever stopping to inquire from whence they come, or by whom invented.

"The usual mode of dressing the buffalo and other skins is by immersing them for a few days under a lye from ashes and water, until the hair can be removed, when they are strained upon a frame or upon the ground, with stakes or pins driven through the edges into the earth, where they remain for several days, with the brains of the buffalo or elk spread upon and over them, and at last finished by 'graining,' as it is termed, by the squaws, who use a sharpened bone, the shoulder-blade, or other large bone of the animal, sharpened at the edge, somewhat like an adze, with the edge of which they scrape the fleshy side of the skin, bearing on it with the weight of their bodies, thereby drying and softening the skin and fitting it for use.

"The greater part of these skins, however, go through still another operation afterward, which gives them a greater value and renders them much more serviceable—that is, the process of smoking. For this a small hole is dug in the

INDIAN CAMP—WOMEN DRESSING AND TANNING SKINS. 1832

ground, and a fire is built in it with rotten wood, which will produce a great quantity of smoke without much blaze, and several small poles of the proper length stuck in the ground around it, and drawn and fastened together at the top around which a skin is wrapped in form of a tent, and generally sewed together at the edges to secure the smoke within it. Within this the skins to be smoked are placed, and in this connection the tent will stand a day or so, inclosing the heated smoke; and by some chemical process or other, which I do not understand, the skins thus acquire a quality which enables them, after being ever so many times wet, to dry soft and pliant as they were before, which secret I have never yet seen practiced in my own country; and for the lack of which, all of our dressed skins, when once wet, are, I think chiefly ruined.

"An Indian's dress of deer skins, which is wet a hundred times upon his back, dries soft; and his lodge also, which stands in the rains and even through the severity of winter, is taken down as soft and clean as when it was first put up.

"A Crow is known wherever he is met by his beautiful white dress, and his tall and elegant figure; the greater part of the men being six feet high. The Blackfeet, on the other hand, are more of the herculean make — about middling stature, with broad shoulders and great expansion of chest; and the skins of which their dresses are made are chiefly dressed black, or of a dark brown color, from which circumstance, in all probability, they, having black leggins or moccasins, have got the name of Blackfeet."

The same writer refers frequently to the skin clothing worn by the Indians, both men and women, as being especially well dressed, as no doubt it was.   Time being of no object to the Indian of that day, the squaws would bestow unlimited labor on choice skins for the making of special costumes, and then as now, elbow grease was the most useful ingredient in tanning.

The African Kaffirs make durable leather, and some creditable work is turned out by the Eskimos who labor under the disadvantage of very low temperatures prevailing much of the time, which always renders dressing slower and more difficult.

Skin dressing tools of hard polished stone often with fair cutting edges and shaped to fit either the hand or a wooden haft, are found in most collections of stone age relics.   Some of these are shaped like the blade of a bowel or round edged adze and were hafted and used in a similar manner, the hide being spread on a piece of level ground, with a portion of it stretched and held firmly between the feet of the operator while it was thinned and softened by chipping strokes.

The woman's knife of the Eskimo of a semi-lunar shape persists in the saddler's knife and the moon knife of the tanner; its only descendant in most households being the kitchen chopping knife.

Although the country abounded with sources of tannic acid, such as the various barks, acorns, etc., their properties seem to have remained as unknown to the native Americans as did those of the various metals. Salt and the alkalies seem to have never been used either, the hair being set by careful drying on skins wanted with the fur on and the softness and pliability in all cases secured by a liberal use of grease, both animal and elbow.

Buckskin, Indian style, is made about as follows: After removing the skin from the deer let it lie in clear water or a mixture of water and ashes until the hair and grain (epidermis) will slip readily. Then remove and throw over a beam where it is first fleshed and then grained with either an iron or hardwood graining knife. The brains have been removed from the head of the deer and boiled for an hour in about a gallon of water.

Let this water stand until it cools so the hand can be held in it, then put in the grained

skin and work continually for two or three minutes by squeezing, wringing and stirring, then
take it out, wring it and pull and stretch in all
directions as it dries. If not soft enough heat up
and put in again, work and dry as before.

If it is still a little hard apply a small
amount of grease, work it in thoroughly and then
smoke it over a fire of dozy or punky wood. Such
half decayed wood is preferred, as it gives off the
maximum amount of smoke with little flame.
Contact with flame or severe heat while smoking
will burn and injure the buckskin.

The Indian method of smoking buckskin by
erecting a pole frame of suitable size and conical
shape, covering it with the skins to be treated,
loosely laced together, and building the fire in
the center gives equally as good results but probably no better than the white man's smoke house.

In dressing fur skins, the hide was fleshed
without the soaking to remove the hair or fur
which was kept as dry and clean as possible.
The skin was stretched out and the brain water
applied several times to the pelt side only. It
was then pulled and rubbed until soft, in much
the same manner as the buckskin. No especial
process was used to cleanse the fur, and as a
consequence it was often greasy at the edges and
more or less dirty and odorous. For this reason
fur skins dressed by the Indian methods are not

much in demand nowadays. There is no doubt, however, that Indian dressed and made skin garments served their purpose admirably when use and not ornament was the end principally desired. Though their handling was defective in many ways such skins would last as long under the hard usage as any, the comparatively light wear and careful treatment given furs among civilized people being chiefly responsible for their long lasting qualities.

It is nothing unusual for rugs, robes, and garment furs to be in use for from twenty to fifty years and remain in good order, but it must be kept in mind that such furs are used only during the coldest months and carefully stored during the remainder of the time, very different from the conditions obtaining in Indian life.

There are some articles of Indian manufacture still on the market, articles for which the more advanced civilization seems not to have produced a duplicate. Probably because the labor involved seems so much out of proportion to the results. The manufacture of Indian Robes is so interesting that it has been made the subject of our next chapter.

CHAPTER VII.

THE writer's first recollections of a fur robe, over forty years ago, are of a peculiar smelling woolly "Buffalo" hide, which he was told had been tanned by the Indians. It was sold in the East for $5.00, and had probably been purchased with a pint or so of diluted alcohol. Until the practical extermination of the buffalo the Indian dressed robes held the market, and a better protection from cold and storm has never been found.

The scarcity of large fur bearers and the cheapness of heavy woven blankets have lessened the demand for fur robes, but a few examples of native work are still sold and in use. Some of the most notable of these are the robes of guanaco and vicuna skins made by the natives of Patagonia, South America.

The skins of the guanaco, a wild variety of the llama, are chiefly used, and are sewed with sinew in wonderfully even stitches. The oil dressed skins are prone to crack and the sinew to stiffen with age until it becomes like fine wire but the native plan of joining the skins is calcu-

74

lated to reduce the waste to a minimum and en-
title the makers true conservationists.

Rows of skins joined head to tail are alter-
nated across the width of the robe, as the woolly
pelt makes it unnecessary to run it all the same
way. By this method the entire skin of the body
and legs is utilized, any tabs and scraps trimmed
off being used to fill out the edges. Sometimes
a narrow border of a darker variety is added, and
robes of the softer fur of the vicuna are also made
by the same people.

Such robes as these are quite valuable, and
when furnished with a light cloth lining are well
suited for carriage wraps or couch covers. They
make fine camp blankets, light and warm, and
are in demand for bed covers in the scattered
ranch houses of Patagonia.

The Eskimo where in contact with whites
make some robes chiefly of seal skins. Quite
elaborate patterns are sometimes worked out in
these using pieces of skin in contrasting colors.
It is said that the Boethicks, natives of Newfoundland, owe their extinction to the robes and
clothing of valuble furs which they were so skill-
ful in taking and preparing.

The unprincipled white adventurers and
trappers of an early day found it easier and more
remunerative to shoot down and rob them than
to capture the fur bearers themselves, and a weak

and inoffensive tribe was hunted and harried out of existence before any adequate protection could be given them.

A peculiar form of fur robe known as the Rabbit Skin Blanket is still made occasionally by the Indians of some parts of Canada. The best description of its mode of manufacture and use has been written by a former employee of the Hudson Bay Company, Martin Hunter, to whom we are indebted for the following:

"Some thirty years ago many of the Indians along the northern shores of Huron and Superior, Lake of the Woods and on to the Red River and away up in the far North, not only used rabbit-skin blankets or robes, but also coats, skirts, caps, etc., made from the skins of these little animals. Young children being clothed from head to foot, cap, coat, pants, mitts, and socks all being made of rabbit-skins, and thus dressed they could stay out of doors and face the most extreme cold with impunity.

"In the olden days a blanket made out of rabbit-skins was traded at our shops for one of equal size of imported wool. The young generation, however, are above either making or using the home-made blanket, the construction of which is fast becoming one of the lost arts.

"A blanket the size of a H. B. blanket, 3½ point, i. e., five feet six inches long by five feet broad, required the skins of sixty rabbits, and a blanket of the 4 point size, i. e., 6½ feet long by 6 feet broad, requires 10 skins.

"Winter skins only are used, and as skinned from day to day. They are kept out in the frost until such time as the good wife of the tepee decides to cut them up into strips.

"The skins are first opened up the belly and are flattened out like coon skins. When the required number are at this stage, the woman or young girl begins cutting. She varies the breadth of the strips according to the part of the skins she is at that time cutting. The belly or thin portion in breadths of an inch and the back or thick part of the hide one-half inch wide. Each skin properly cut should give a length of from fifteen to eighteen feet long.

"As each skin is cut the strip is either baled or folded in a short coil, squeezed close together and placed in a cool, damp place, and so on till the required number of skins are finished.

"A frame is made of four dry peeled poles crossed at the four corners and tied securely. The size of the square is from four to six inches larger at top and sides than the proposed blanket is to be. It is then propped up against the shack or a tree at an angle and a backing of number nine twine is secured around the inside of the frame about four inches from the poles. The

backing or cord is kept in place by being laced
to the poles with smaller twine and then it is
ready to take on the skins

"The looping of the strips is worked from
side to side. A slight twist is given to the strips
as the work goes on. The smaller the loop or
mesh the heavier the blanket, and consequently
a greater number of skins are required.

"When these blankets were in general use the
Indians had light weight ones for spring and
heavy ones for the winter.

"Some of the women used long, narrow,
wood needles such as net needles to carry the
strands when weaving, but the majority simply
worked up the strips by hand, giving as I have
said a slight twist to the strand as each loop or
mesh is made. This gives it a ropy appearance,
which makes the hair stand out all around. Each
time the edge is arrived at, the strip is passed
over twice. This gives it strength, and makes
with the twine a strong border to the rug.

After the blanket is completed, allow it to
remain in the frame for a day or two to dry, then
unlace the small twine you had to keep it in place
and the blanket falls out, ready for use.

Notwithstanding you can shove your thumb
or two or three fingers through the loops or mesh-
es, it alone is warmer than several woolen blankets. The three objections to a rabbit-skin

blanket are: it is bulky, heavy, and the hairs come out continually, but when one is in the bush they generally wear old, greasy clothes, and don't worry about their being covered with hairs so long as they sleep warm.

It is hardly to be credited the degree of cold one can withstand when using one of these blankets or sleeping bags. When one travels with dog-teams, the weight and bulk of the blanket is not of so much consequence, but when one has to back-pack their requirements, a bush man prefers to freeze a little at nights rather than to be overloaded.

Sleeping bags are made of rabbit-skins for the company's employees who travel long distances by dog-team in the far North. From the feet up to the chest it is sewed all the way. The man slips his legs into this, resumes a recumbent position and laces it up to his chin. Attached to the back is a hood. This he adjusts on his head before lacing up, and there he is with only a small portion of the face exposed.

My first enlightenment as to the warmth of a rabbit-skin bag was on Lake Nepigon. I was traveling in February with two half breeds from the shore of Lake Superior. One of the days we were on Lake Nepigon it was bitterly cold. Night was coming on apace and we had to reluctantly camp at the lea of Gros Lap, a wind swept point in the body of the Lake. Amongst the debris of rocks which had fallen down from the side we managed to find a space sufficiently large to make our fire and spread a few branches for our bed.

Charles de Laroud, one of my men, said he was not going to sleep in a hole like that but would take his bag after supper and sleep on the ice. I looked at him in amazement and said he would certainly freeze. It was clear moonlight and I saw him walk out fifty yards from the shore, get into his bag, drop onto the ice, whistle his dogs about him, and that was the last of Charlie until next morning when he arose, walked to shore, came into the fire circle and smiled quite serenely.

Though I had a pair of heavy H. B. blankets and a fire was kept up all night, sleep for me was only by short intervals at a time. At daylight I took reading of my thermometer and found it registered 38 below zero, which was a pretty severe test to the rabbit-skin bag. Although Charles had passed ten hours out on the ice he assured me he never felt cold. On reaching Nepigon post I secured a rabbit-skin bag for myself and on the balance of the trip north found its value.

Some of the post people use rabbit-skin blankets in the houses as quilts or bed spreads, but they cover them with some fancy print to prevent the hairs spreading out.

Large sized blankets at the present day cost from seven to ten dollars each, and by writing to the Hudson Bay's Agent at either Fort Williams, Lake Superior; Montizambets, Lake Superior; or Nepigon House, Lake Superior, one might be secured, but time would have to be given for its manufacture, as they are not kept for sale."

Having handled these blankets (though never used them) I should say there is little doubt as to their warmth and lightness, but their inclination to shed hair would hardly commend them to most housekeepers. Dressing the skins before weaving would hardly prevent this, as the fur of the native rabbit has little durability. Perhaps if the skins were stretched and treated with some preservative they might be basted together and enclosed between covers of light cloth as a layer of cotton or wool is, in making bed comforts. Tying this at frequent intervals would keep the fur filling in place. Where rabbits abound this plan would be worth trying and the expense would be small, rabbit skins being worth hardly more than a cent apiece.

The H. B. Indians use the skins of the Northern Varying or White Hare, but presume those of the Cottontail or Jack Rabbit could be worked in a similar manner.

The natives of Central America and those of Hawaii at one time made most beautiful feather robes, but it is doubtful if any of them are produced at the present time.   Those made in Hawaii were so rare that only royalty ever possessed them.

CHAPTER VIII.

TOOLS AND APPLIANCES FOR TANNING AND DRESSING.

THE older methods of dressing furs, before the introduction of machinery, followed about the same program as at the present time, but was carried on by foot and hand power exclusively. Now, however, most fur dressing shops supplied with power contain:

Washing Tanks, of wire revolving in a tank of water.

Dryers, or Whizzers, wire baskets revolving very rapidly to throw the moisture out of the skins.

Cleaning Drums, to extract the grease with dry and heated sawdust.

Beating Drums, to remove the dust from the fur.

Beaming Mills, for thinning skins.

Tramping or Pounding Machines, for softening skins.

Drying Chambers, where the air is kept in motion with fans, besides many other tools for hand work.

I shall endeavor to give details of the most important of these as they chiefly concern the dresser on a small scale.

THE BEAɈ.   One or more of these is neces-
sɈry and can be made of a hardwood slab about
36 inches long, hinged to an upright so as to be
adjustable or fixed at an angle of about 45 degrees.

A good Beam is frequently made of a slab or

log about seven
feet long, fitted
with two legs
two feet from
o n e e n d a n d
with the other
resting on the
floor.   Another
form is merely

A LOG FUR BEAM

spiked on top of two upright posts of the proper
heighth.   It is well to have two beams, one much
smaller than the other to suit large and small
skins.

TUBS.   For soaking, washing and pickling
skins several half barrels, lard or butter tubs will
answer the purpose of vats.   They should be of
wood, for all operations except washing or soaking with gasoline or benzine.

KNIVES.   Fleshing, also called beaming or
breaking knives.   There are a number of styles
in this tool, such as the small single edge, large
double edge and the combination smooth Ɉnd

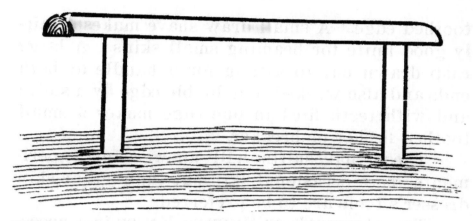

FUR BEAM, NOT ADJUSTABLE. GOOD FOR TWO MEN
OR LARGE HIDES

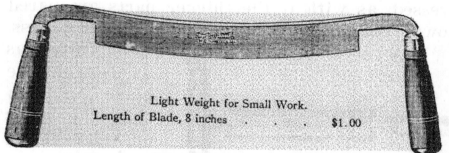

Light Weight for Small Work.
Length of Blade, 8 inches   .   .   . $1.00

FLESHING KNIFE—SMALL SINGLE EDGE

FLESHING KNIFE—DOUBLE EDGE

FLESHING KNIFE—SMOOTH AND TOOTHED

toothed edge. A small draw shave makes a fair-
ly good knife for beaming small skins. A large
rasp drawn out to a tang for a handle at both
ends and also worked to a double edge by a smith
and with teeth filed in one edge makes a small
toothed flesher or breaker.

These makeshifts will answer for experiments or an occasional skin but the regular skin
dresser's tools are to be preferred.

THE CURRIER'S OR SKIVING KNIFE is a necessity when any but the lightest skins are to be
dressed, as with it the thicker parts are pared
down, reducing skins to a uniform thickness.

CURRIER OR SKIVING KNIFE

This knife has
a detachable
blade on each
side, the edges
of which are
ground as one
would a chisel
and afterward
turned over at a right angle by the use of a turning steel made for that purpose. This knife
works after the manner of a plane, cutting off a
shaving at each stroke, thick or thin according to
the depth of the turned edge. Considerable practice will be necessary to use this tool without in-
flicting ugly cuts on an inoffensive skin, and it
is necesary to sharpen the blade frequently from

time to time with the small finger steel, as the crystals of salt in a skin soon take the keen edge off.

When not in use, all steel tools should be kept heavily oiled to prevent rusting. A small skin may be scraped with a hand scraper and shaved down with a shoe knife or small draw shave on a half round piece of wood, bolted or screwed to the work table top. These small tools are also necessary to work around the heads, feet and tails of large skins.

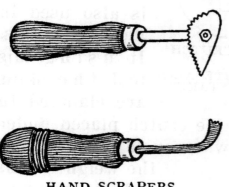

HAND SCRAPERS
Made of Shave Hook and Screw-driver.

A fair hand scraper may be made by heating the blade of a screw driver, hammering it out broad and bending it at right angles like a hoe blade. Use a file to make small teeth on the blade. A plumber's shave-hook may have similar teeth filed along one side and be used for the same purpose.

A substitute for the skiving knife is not easily made, though for small skins a wood scraper blade ground and the edge turned may be sufficient.

For breaking up and softening the partly
dry skins a dull fleshing knife is sometimes used
also the crutch
or moon knife
and the staking
knife. The moon
knife, consist-
ing of a circu-
lar steel blade
clamped to a
crutch shaped
wooden handle
is also used in
fleshing skins.
In using this
tool the skins
are clamped in

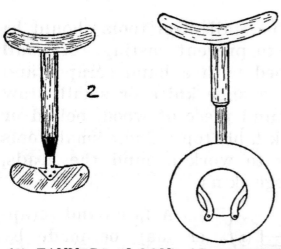

(1) TANNERS "MOON" OR CRUTCH
KNIFE.
(2) HOME MADE SUBSTITUTE AL-
SO CALLED "SHOULDER STAKE"

a stretching frame and the crutch placed under
armpit of the operator who can in this way use
the weight of his
body in the pro-
cess. The blade
of an ordinary
kitchen chopping
knife may be
hafted and used
in a similar way.

THE STRETCH-
ING FRAME con-

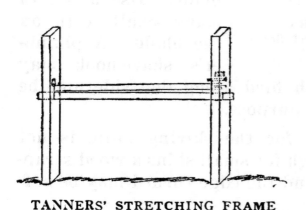

TANNERS' STRETCHING FRAME

sists of two uprights connected by a crosspiece, with a second crosspiece hinged at one end, arranged to clamp tightly on the first. It may be either a fixture or portable, but should be made of stiff scantlings 2 x 4 in size at least. The porable frame is leaned against the wall when in use.

A STAKE KNIFE for stretching skins, has for

a foundation a piece of two inch plank about 12 by 24 inches with a three foot upright mortised and braced in the center and fitted at the top with a piece of steel (saw blade) about five or six inches square, the corners slightly rounded.

STAKE KNIFE FOR
"BREAKING" SKINS

Unlike the leather maker the tanner and dresser of furs uses no splitting machines on account of the fur roots, but must reduce their thickness by other means. Emery or sandpaper are used on power driven wheels and by hand. Sandpaper can be glued to the surface of a curved block of wood and the same fastened in a vise where the skin is drawn back and forth over it. The block should be of two inch wood, six to ten

inches square with a crosspiece screwed to the
back to provide a hold for the vise or the hand.

DRU N.   When a number of skins are to be
cleaned some kind of a drum is necessary. Those
used in the large shops are about four feet wide
and about six or eight feet in diameter.   The
cleaning drums have either several shelves six
inches wide or the same number of rows of wood-
en pegs, on the interior circumference.   A num-

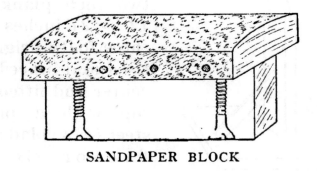

SANDPAPER BLOCK

ber of skins with a quantity of very fine dry hardwood sawdust is placed in the drum and after
revolving steadily for three or four hours at
about twenty revolutions per minute the fur will
be clean and soft but full of sawdust.

The beating drums of similar size with wood-
en ends and sides of $\frac{1}{4}$-inch mesh wire cloth are
supplied with wire mesh shelves which catch the
skins and carry them nearly to the top whence
they drop against the wire cloth covering the
drum's circumference thus cleansing the fur of

sawdust. Both cleaning and beating drums are often enclosed in wooden closets, the former heated by steam pipes or charcoal that the grease and oil may be extracted and the latter to prevent the sawdust flying about.

CLEANING DRUMS AS USED IN LARGE ESTABLISHMENTS

For hand work a barrel or box placed on an axle with crank attached has been found to work well in cleaning. An opening fitted with a cover is made in one side through which the skin with a quantity of sawdust is thrown in, the cover clamped on, and the barrel revolved, so as to keep the contents moving. A box hung by the corners like a type of churn once popular would insure a thorough agitation of the skins and sawdust.

For a hand beating drum I would recommend one made with octagonal heads and covered with wire cloth. Large skins are best beaten with rattans and an ordinary woven wire bed spring will hold them nicely during the process, letting the

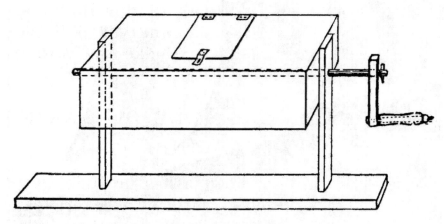

FUR DRUM MADE OF BOX

dust fall through. The furniture beaters supplied by the stores are suitable for small skins.

THE TRAMPING MACHINE consists of two wooden hammers, which are moved alternately up and down and back and forth, in a suitable receptacle, stirring the skins constantly and developing by friction the necessary heat to render them soft and pliable. Before beginning this operation any skins not naturally fat or oily are greased with some animal fat.

The original method, which is still practiced for the choicest pelts is termed Tubbing. In this a tub or half hogshead placed on the floor, slightly inclined, has a number of oiled skins with usually a small amount of sawdust put in it. The workman with barefeet takes his place in the tub and ties around his waist a piece of heavy cloth or bagging already fastened about the top of the tub. This serves to retain the heat and prevent the dust from flying about during the two or three hours treading and twisting necessary to thoroughly soften or leather the skins.

A clothes pounder or washerwoman's "dolly" may be made to take the place of the feet in the softening or Tubbing process. Twisting, wringing and rubbing with the hands as in washing clothes will serve the same purpose, but it is a tiresome process and one for which the hand seems hardly suited.

COMBS of at least two sizes will be needed by the dresser to put the fur in order and straighten any tangles. They are made of steel, brass and german silver. The steel is the cheapest and must be kept well oiled to prevent rusting which the other metals are not so liable to. A coarse and fine combination comb is made which is very

handy. Robe combs, resembling an infant garden rake, are suitable for the largest skins.

Much experimental work can be done with
very few tools and very creditable work too, but
improved appliances and especially those run by
power do certainly lessen the drudgery of skin
dressing and enable a few hands to turn out a
vast volume of well finished furs in a short time.

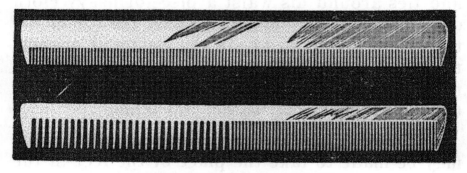

FURRIERS' STEEL COMBS

Tramping and Beating and Cleaning Machines handle large quantities of skins at once
and even then do not require the operators entire
attention, and though skins so treated may need
some hand labor in addition to complete the processes, the machines take care of the great bulk of
it.

Your good right arm and a rattan will beat
a skin as well as the electric beater, if you don't
get tired too soon. A delicate skin can be softened and leathered better by the human hands and

feet than by any machines devised to date. Good hand tools are not very expensive and will great- ly expedite the dressing of ordinary skins.

The Eskimo women soften skins frequently by chewing them an appetizing process which we will hardly care to emulate, however efficacious it may be.

CHAPTER IX.

A S has been already explained the dressing of fur skins is quite different from the process of tanning leather or proper tanning. So too, the materials used are very different in most cases.

In leather tanning, extracts or infusions are often made use of from various barks and leaves, but the action of such is quite slow, being a matter of weeks or even months before the skins immersed in such tan liquors are completely tanned.

Another objection to the use of barks, etc., is the fact that such material often contains also considerable coloring matter, usually brown, which would affect the fur put in it. In some instances this is not undesirable, such as dressing sheep skins for linings, etc. By concentrating the vegetable extracts the process of tanning will be reduced especially for light skins.

Some of the barks containing the most tannin are: White Ash; White, Red, Chestnut and in fact all varieties of the Oaks; Sumac; Hemlock. and Chestnut. Acorns and the leaves of these trees also contain much tannin. Mayweed, Sweetfern, Smartweed and Alfalfa may be used for the same purpose.

To prepare for use the barks, leaves or plants are broken, cut or ground into small pieces and then left to steep or leach in water to extract the strength. Terra Japonica also known as Catechu is much used in tanning but it also contains much brown dye. Salt is universally used in preparing skins either by itself or in combination with other things. The coarse form is commonly used on account of the lower price, fine salt can be used for all similar purposes and is to be preferred for rubbing on skins in the powdered form or for making pastes for application to the flesh sides of skins. Salt opens the pores of the hide, and lets in the tan and prevents decomposition of the skin.

Alum is probably one of the first mineral agents to be used in fur dressing. It is an astringent, sets the hair and epidermis, and with other ingredients helps to render the skin impervious to water. Alum, however, hardens and shrinks a skin, both of which qualities are the opposite of what is desired. Its great disadvantage lies in its plumping or thickening properties. An alum cured skin shaved and thinned down from the inside and then replaced in a salt and alum bath, for a day or two, will be found on removal to have plumped up to nearly its original thickness.

If two freshly salted skins of the same kind of animal are placed at the same time, one in a salt and alum solution and the other in an acid tan and left there a week or so the difference will be readily apparent. The alum cured skin will be stiff and harsh, the other not increased in thickness and more pliable than when put in and will require but a comparatively short time to beam and thin down. It is almost impossible to dress out the fur of some animals, to look fluffy and natural after immersion in an alum solution and it is apt to leave any hair stiff, dry and without gloss.

In the case of half spoiled specimens, alum will save the day if anything will. Some times an animal will be received in the flesh on which the hair is starting to slip. If it pulls out easily on any part of the body and limbs it is too late, but if only the lower part of the abdomen seems disposed to slough, quick work and plenty of alum may save it in very fair condition.

Except in the case of rare or valuable specimens this is not to be advised as the handling of such skins in the first stages of decay is always more or less dangerous. Such skins should be snatched off without delay and immersed in a strong, warm solution of salt and alum. The

RAW SKINS PALE AND LOW GRADE

(1) Small Opossum, Open; (2) Small Muskrat, Open; (3) Medium Muskrat, Cased; (4) Medium Opossum, Cased.

alum in this acts as a powerful astringent drawing together the fibers around the root of each hair and binding together the cutis and epidermis.

Acids are used in skin dressing to destroy the gluten and also aid in cleaning both fur and hide. Sulphuric and Oxalic are the acids in principal use. Sulphuric is the more violent in action and great care should be used in handling it in a clear state. It should *never* be allowed to come in contact with the hands, clothing or hides before being diluted with water, milk or other liquids.

Dilute Acetic Acid in the form of Vinegar and weak Lactic Acid as sour milk or buttermilk are made use of. Borax and Saltpetre are used to hasten tanning by softening and penetrating the skins in a similar manner to salt and Glaubers Salt.

Lime, Red Arsenic and Wood Ashes or Potash are used to remove hair or fur from skins to be used as leather. Flour and Bran are ingredients in tanner's pastes and liquors. Various combinations of oils and soaps serve to soften tawed skins and in cleaning, Soda, Benzine, Gasoline, Sawdust, Meal and Magnesia serve useful purposes.

In the preparation of skins terms for the various operations have sprung up, which may puzzle the uninitiated; to take them in about their sequence some of them are as follows:

SOAKING, relaxing a cured skin, rendering it flexible enough to be held on the fleshing beam.

FLESHING, removing the muscular inner coat with the bits of flesh, fat, etc., to open up the true skin to chemical action.

GRAINING, removing the hair and epidermis from skins to be made into leather.

PICKLING, soaking in the various tanning or tawing solutions.

SLEEKING, working liquid preparations out of skins by pressure and scraping with tools.

SKIVING or CURRYING, paring or reducing the thickness of skins.

STRETCHING or BREAKING, separating the fibre of a partly dried tawed skin.

STAKING, using the stake knife for breaking or fleshing.

WHIZZING, extracting the moisture by centrifugal action.

TUBBING, softening or leathering tawed skins by working in a tub with the feet or mechanically.

PLUCKING, removing the over or guard hairs of the pelt, usually done immediately after fleshing.

DRUMMING, revolving the skins inside of drums for the purpose (a) removing grease and cleaning the fur, with hot dry sawdust or similar material, and (b) beating or agitating the furs to remove such sawdust remaining in them.

LIMING, soaking in solution of lime in water.

BATING, removing the salts of lime from a skin by acid fermentation.

SAMMING, partly drying skins.

SCOURING, washing.

STRIKING OUT, sleeking or working watery solution out of a skin.

HANDLING, stirring about, working.

Often if the common name of some material is known to us it can be easily procured and at a slight cost. For instance, take the formula used for the salt and alum pickle No. 10. Oxide of Hydrogen 1 Cong., heat to 212 degress and add Sulphate Aluminum and Potassium 165, Chloride of Sodium 45. This is much more intelligible if we say: To a gallon of boiling water add a pound of alum and a quarter pound of salt. Below is a list of

COMMON NAMES OF SOME CHEMICAL SUBSTANCES.

Aqua Fortis—Nitric Acid.

Aqua Regia—Nitro-Muriatic Acid.

Blue Vitrol—Sulphate of Copper.

Cream of Tartar—Bitartrate of Potassium.
Calomel—Chloride of Mercury.
Chalk—Carbonate of Calcium.
Salt of Tartar—Carbonate of Potassa.
Caustic Potassa—Hydrate of Potassium.
Chloroform—Chloride of Gormyle.
Common Salt—Chloride of Sodium.
Copperas or Green Vitrol—Sulphate of Iron.
Corrosive Sublimate — Bichloride of Mer-
cury.
Diamond—Pure Carbon.
Dry Alum—Sulphate of Aluminum and Po-
tassium.
Epsom Salts—Sulphate of Magnesia.
Ethiops Mineral—Black Sulphide of Mer-
cury.
Fire Damp—Light Carbureted Hydrogen.
Galena—Sulphide of Lead.
Glauber Salt—Sulphate of Soda.
Glucose—Grape Sugar.
Goulard Water—Basic Acetate of Lead.
Iron Pyrites—Bisulphide of Iron.
Jewelers' Putty—Oxide of Tin.
King Yellow—Sulphide of Arsenic.
Laughing Gas—Protoxide of Nitrogen.
Lime—Oxide of Calcium.
Lunar Caustic—Nitrate of Silver.
Mosia Gold—Bisulphide of Tin.
Muriate of Lime—Chloride of Calcium.

Niter of Saltpetre—Nitrate of Potash.
Oil of Vitrol—Sulphuric Acid.
Potash—Oxide of Potassium.
Red Lead—Oxide of Lead.
Rust of Iron—Oxide of Iron.
Sal Ammoniac—Muriate of Ammonia.
Slacked Lime—Hydrate of Calcium.
Soda—Oxide of Sodium.
Spirits of Hartshorn—Ammonia
Spirit of Salt — Hydrochloric of Muriatic
    Acid.
Stucco, or Plaster Paris—Sulphate of Lime.
Sugar of Lead—Acetate of Lead.
Verdegris—Basic Acetate of Copper.
Vermilion—Sulphide of Mercury.
Vinegar—Acetic Acid (diluted).
Volatile Alkali—Ammonia.
Water—Oxide of Hydrogen.
White Precipitate—Ammoniated Mercury.
White Vitrol—Sulphate of Zinc.

CHAPTER X.

No. 1.

ALUM TAWING SOLUTIONS.

Salt ....¼ lb.
Alum, crystals or powdered..1 lb.
Water ....1 gal.

Heat to dissolve the salt and alum and when luke warm or cold immerse the skins.

No. 2.

Water ....1 gal.
Salt .... (about 1¾ lb.) 1 qt.
Alum .... (about 1   lb.) 1 pt.

Heat to boiling and cool.

No. 3.

Water, warm ......1 gal. and add
Bran ....1 qt.

Allow to stand in a warm room 24 hours or until it ferments, then heat and add

Salt ....1 lb. or 1 pt.
Alum ....1 lb.

Let cool before putting the fleshed skins in.

105

No. 4.

BARK SOLUTION.

To prepare this, fill a pot or kettle half full of bark ground or broken into small chips and then fill with water and steep until the strength is extracted, to simmer it for about three hours is best, add about two ounces to the gallon if the skins have been salted or four if not. The stronger the solution the quicker the action, but it will be well to allow three weeks at least to tan.

No. 5.

DRY TANNING TO BE APPLIED TO THE FLESH SIDE ONLY OF SKINS.

Alum ....2½ lb.
Salt ....1 lb.
Oatmeal..........1 lb. (or flour)

All finely powdered and dissolved in enough sour milk or buttermilk to the consistency of cream. Coat the flesh side.

No. 6.

Alum ....1 lb.
Saltpetre ....1 lb.
Salt ....2 lbs.

Mix thoroughly and sprinkle on the flesh side evenly.

No. 7

Water ....1 gal.
Alum ....2½ lb.
Salt ....1 lb.

Heat the water to dissolve, and when cool brush on the flesh side of the dampened skin.

Any of the solutions used to immerse skins in may be brushed on the flesh side in this way. Lay the skins flesh sides together in pairs or if a single skin, double it up flesh in and leave in a cool place. Repeat this dressing of paste or liquid once or twice a day for two or three days, the point being to keep it damp with the chemicals until they penetrate.

A rather strong sulphuric acid solution is often used in this way, and I will give two formulas for this.

No. 8.

Water ....2 qts.
Salt .... .1 lb.
Sulphuric Acid........1 oz. (fluid)

No. 9.

Water ....1 qt.
Salt ....4 oz.
Sulphuric Acid ....1 oz.

Dissolve salt in water first then add the acid.

The No. 9 will, if the skin is well soaked, tan light or thin skins in about twelve hours, or over night. The No. 8 requires about twenty-eight hours for the same skins. I would not care to recommend these strong acid solutions if they are left in the leather without washing out or neutralizing, as they are liable to shorten the life of the same.

Some directions for dressing furs caution never to wet the fur side; that is all nonsense. They have all of them been wet hundreds of times on the animals' backs without hurt and almost without exception they need cleaning before they are fit for use as clothing for civilized people. Immersion in preservative or tanning solutions also tend to curb the enthusiasm of moths and such destructive insects for using the finished product as a bill of fare.

Long continued soaking in some of these pickles does not injure a skin in the least, as taxidermists often use their jars of sulphuric or alum pickle to store skins for weeks and months, in some cases years. Personally I prefer the following:

No. 10.

SULPHURIC TAN LIQUOR.

Water ....1 gal.
Salt ....1 qt.
Sulphuric Acid.   1 oz. (fluid)

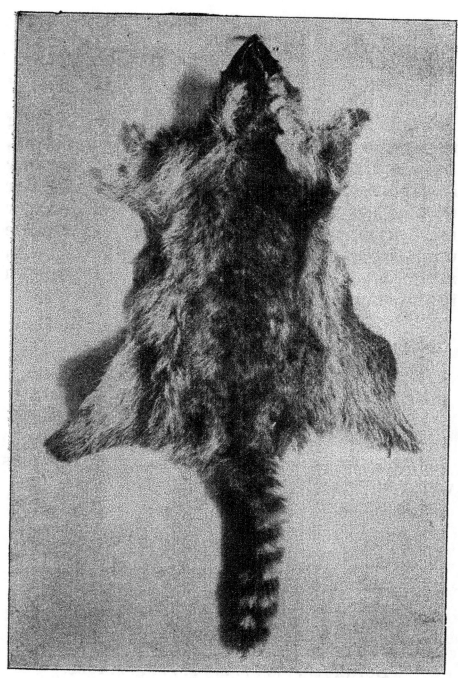

RAW RACCOON SKIN — AVERAGE SOUTHEAST SECTIONS

Bring water to boiling to dissolve the salt, and cool before adding acid.

Don't lean over it while pouring and stirring the acid in; the fumes are not specially beneficial. As many skins may be put in as it will cover readily, but the strength will be about spent after tanning say about one skin the size of a fox or raccoon to each two quarts of the liquor made up. Keep it in wood, earthen or glass ware, *never metal.* Alum solution No. 2 may be used in the same way.

No. 11.

OXALIC ACID TAN LIQUOR.

Water ....1 gal.
Salt ....1 pt.
Oxalic Acid (pulverized)....2 oz.

This is especially adapted to light skins which will tan in six to twenty-four hours.

No. 12.

SULPHURIC ACID WITH MILK.

Sour Buttermilk ....1 gal.
Water ....1 gal.
Salt ....1½ lbs.
Saltpetre ....2 oz.
Borax ....1 oz.
Sulphuric Acid ....8 oz.

DRESSED GREY FOX SKIN—AVERAGE SOUTHEAST
SECTIONS

111

Dissolve the salt, saltpetre and borax in the water, add the buttermilk and last of all the acid, stirring well. Put the soaked and fleshed skins in this and stir them about every hour or so for three or four hours for light skins. When tanned remove, wring and wash out.

Washing solutions are varied, but for washing out acid liquors should contain some alkali like soda which neutralizes any acid remaining in the skin. Use to a pail of water a handful of washing soda. Some take ½ lb. soap, 2 ounces soda to the pail of lukewarm water. Rinse afterwards in clear water. It is a good plant to put the skin on the beam and "sleek" it with a dull fleshing knife or a piece of hard wood or metal, that is, scrape over it, pressing the liquid out ahead of the tool. This helps clear and open the pores.

It is impossible to give the exact treatment for any given skin, being governed by the dresser's personal ideas and the state of the individual skin, both of which naturally vary much.

To dress a skin by an application to the flesh side only would call for a program something like that in the first column, while the second would show about what the skin immersed in an acid liquor would undergo. If the dry dressed skin was very fat it would require another round of the sawdust and beating drums.

No. 1
Soak.
Flesh.
Pickle.
Dry.
Oil.
Stretch.
Drum.
Stretch.
Drum.
Beat.

No. 2
Soak.
Flesh.
Pickle.
Wash.
Rinse.
Gasoline.
Drum.
Beat.
Stretch.
Oil.
Drum.
Beat.

Fat skins in the second treatment would require a degreasing soak in gasoline after fleshing and before pickling.

For making buckskin the hair is removed before tanning and frequently an unprime or damaged skin of a furbearer can be utilized by making into leather. The most common soak to remove hair or fur is made in the following proportion:

No. 13.

Water ....5 gals.
Slacked Lime ....4 qts.
Hardwood Ashes ....4 qts.

The fresh or relaxed skins are left in this one to six days, until the hair or fur starts readily. A more rapid acting application is made of

No. 14.

Water ....1 qt.
Red Arsenic ....1 lb.
Unslacked Lime ....1 lb.

Boil the water and arsenic, let it cool and add the lime. Paint this on the flesh side of a skin, (fresh or soaked), fold it together and let it lie 12 or 15 hours, when the hair will probably be ready to scrape off. Unfortunately nothing has been concocted, to date, which will make fur grow on a skin either raw or dressed.

There are many, many more formulas for fur tanning, most of which will produce fair results when combined with two ingredients, common sense and elbow grease, and without those any of the foregoing will be useless.

Some people still retain the idea that there is some magical powder or chemical with which a skin may be sprinkled or saturated that will render it at once and forever soft and pliable, something as the photo developer brings out the image on the exposed negative. Would that it were so, but the best that has been done so far is to discover materials that are quicker acting and to transfer part of the most severe and monotonous work to machines.

CHAPTER XI.

SKINS which have been just taken off need no soaking, as the object of it is to soften and relax them so they may be flattened on the beam for fleshing, or the removal of the inner muscular coat. Most tanning liquors will relax a dried skin but it will take much longer than when clear water or a special soak is used.

Using the tan liquid to soak unfleshed skins weakens it considerably, as there is quite an amount of muscle, fat, etc., to absorb it, besides the skin proper. Thin and weak skins it is often necessary to treat so, however.

In cool weather skins may be soaked in clear water, but as even then they require close watching and should not be left long in a damp state, a weak salt solution is best to use. One of the best is for, say, four skins the size of fox or raccoon. Use:

Water ....4 gal.
Borax ....½ oz.
Soap ....1 oz.
Salt ....½ pint
Sulphuric Acid ....¾ fluid oz.

Before adding dissolve the soap in ½ pint of water (or use ½ pt. soft soap). If the skins have been salted the salt may be omitted. The acid aids in setting the hair; do not use if the skin is wanted without hair for leather. Mix thoroughly and immerse skins two to six hours.

When desired, skins may be softened and in fact completely dressed without wetting the fur, though this is hardly practical with work of any amount, and I think most skins are benefitted by the thorough cleansing they get in the various wet solutions. To soak or relax a flat or open skin without wetting the fur, brush the flesh side all over with either the solution given or one made by dissolving a good handful of salt in a pail of water. Saturate a quantity of sawdust with the soak and laying the skin on bench or floor, flesh side up, cover it with the damp sawdust. A cased skin should be laid on a layer of damp sawdust and completely covered with the same. The sawdust must contain enough moisture so that a few drops may be squeezed from a handful.

On the inside of sundried skins will be found a tough, glazed surface which must be cut and scraped away after a little soaking so that the liquor may enter and thoroughly relax the skin. As good a plan as any is to put a number of skins to soak and take them out and partially flesh them one after the other, replacing in the soak until entirely softened.

Thorough relaxation and fleshing is essential to good dressing, as it opens the pores and makes them accessible to the solutions used.

BEAMING AND PLUCKING BEAVER SKINS
(Plucking is Pulling Out the Long or Guard Hairs)

To flesh, throw a skin on the end of the beam and by pressing against it with the chest, hold it in place while by shoving the fleshing knife from you the inner muscular skin with adhering flesh and fat is removed. Some direct that the fleshing be from the tail toward the head, so as to run the right way of the hair roots, but this can hardly be necessary; the skin should be stretched in all directions both side and lengthways. Use a toothed flesher to break the glaze on large dry skins, then soak till they can be fleshed and stretched. Light skins are sometimes pounded before soaking to hasten the process.

The stretching may be done on the stretching frame, and if the skin dries during the process dampen it by brushing the flesh side with either water or soaking or tanning pickle. Skins dampened with the pickles may be safely left for some time in that condition, but if soaked in clear water they should be either dried out or put in tan or the hair may soon slip, especially in warm weather.

Fresh skins should be salted for a day or two before fleshing, as then the salt will have hardened the tissues so the knife will take hold of them better.

The method of using a draw-knife and pulling it toward the operator is not a good one, as it is necessary to hold the skin by driving an awl through it into the beam, thus punching the skin full of awl holes or tearing it. The head, feet and any places not accessible with the large flesher are attended to with hand scrapers and a small knife.

Skins which are to be plucked are treated to that process now, after washing clear in warm soap water. Use one-half pound of soap and two ounces of washing soda in a bucket of water at about 90 degrees for this washing. Wring out and shake to dry the fur but keep the skin damp. Some tack the skin to a board, fur out, and dry it in the sun or near a fire. When the fur is dry try if the overhair will pull out readily. If not keep the back of skin damp until it does, brushing it with clear water if it gets dry.

When the over-hairs start easily, cover the beam with a firm pad of several thicknesses of blanket or something similar and put the skin on it fur up. Then with the fleshing knife rub out most of the over-hairs by careful working. Powdered chalk is sometimes sprinkled on the hair first. Any hairs not removed by this are pulled out by hand. Protect the right thumb with a rubber cot and taking a dull knife in that hand, draw the skin over the edge of a table or board and as the long hairs come into view grasp them between the protected thumb and knife blade and pull them out with a quick jerk.

Skins that seem very greasy may be rid of it by soaking now for an hour in gasoline, wringing out of it and hanging in the air to dry before placing in the tan. Regular fur dressers depend mostly on repeated and lengthy "drumming" to clean skins as benzine or gasoline is quite expensive and the wastage is considerable, but for the amateur without power machines it will prove of great assistance.

The large dry cleaning establishments, redistill dirty gasoline and recover it as clean as ever but for our purpose a few settling cans will answer, as if it stands for a few hours most of the dirt will be precipitated and the comparative clean liquid may be poured off. Water also being heavier than gasoline will take its place at the bottom of the can, but oils and fats combine more or less with the volatile liquid. Gasoline used for cleaning white furs may be used again on dark ones and again for the de-greasing before tanning. For the cleaning after tanning it may be used repeatedly, as but little grease should be present then.

CHAPTER XII.

THE dressing or tanning of furs may be roughly separated into three stages, the first of which is the soaking, fleshing, etc., which tends to open the pores and made quick and ready action of tanning chemicals possible. In the second, the glue is dissolved, the fibres separated and the hair set by these substances. In many cases they also help to clean the skins by cutting the albumen and oil of blood and grease among the fur. The subsequent washing carries off much of this as well as salts and acids, which if left in the pores of the skin would impair its usefulness.

The final treatment is the softening and cleaning which may be described in one word, *work*. In order that a skin may be equally soft in all parts it should be approximately of the same thickness all over, so the hide along the back, back of the neck and at other spots must be thinned by knife, sandpaper or other means. Thin skins are often left till now after the tawing for this, as there is but little to be removed from them while large thick hides should be

121

shaved down before beginning or at least before
completing the tawing process. Frequently they
are taken out of the liquor after a short immersion and partly thinned, returned and again removed to complete the shaving.

SHAVING MINK SKINS IN A LARGE ESTABLISHMENT

The first step on freeing a skin from the
liquor should be to spread it and hang on a line
or frame in a dry, airy place until the moisture
is partly out. If left to themselves fur skins will
contract and shrink in drying, the fibres binding

and gripping together making the whole skin stiff and unfit for use. This should be prevented by pulling and stretching the skin in all directions when half dry and keeping up the process until it is fully dried out, with the fibres in such a condition that a piece of the hide may be stretched in first one way and then another. Small skins may be laid on the beam with a pad underneath them and stretched with the fleshing knife, and large ones taken to the stretching frame, where the operator puts his weight into the operation of the crutch knife or in some cases to the stake knife, which performs a similar part in breaking up and loosening the fibre.

If the skin is to be cleaned with benzine or gasoline it should be soaked now for thirty minutes to an hour, wrung out and put in a cleaning drum or cleaned by hand in a tray or tub. The dust from veneer saws is the best but any fine hardwood sawdust may be used, and common corn meal answers very well. Without a drum the meal should be heated quite warm and put in a box or tub with the skin or skins. Stir and roll the skins about until the fur is completely filled with the meal, then shake and beat it out, repeat the process until the fur is dry and fluffy.

Stretch the skin again and then coat the inside of it with an oil or oil dressing of some sort to complete the softening, and replace the natural uncombined oil which has been in great part extracted. There are almost as many oil dressings as fur dressers, and we will not attempt to enumerate them all. Usually they are composed in great part of animal fats and oils, but some advocate using mineral oil sometimes. Some of the best compositions for this purpose are:

OIL DRESSING RECIPES

(a)

Soft Soap ....1 pt.
Neatsfoot Oil ....1 pt.
Alcohol ....½ pt.

Mix and rub into the flesh side.

(b)

Yolk of Egg.................8 oz.
Glycerin ....4 oz.

Apply sparingly and rub in well.

(c)

Tallow.............. Equal parts
Neatsfoot Oil........

Apply a good coat, about as thick as the hide, hang up till dry, then scrape off the grease and apply a thin coat of solution of soft soap. Let stand twenty-four hours, then scrape well and clean. This is good for heavy robe skins.

(d)

Yellow Soap ....2 parts
Fine Oatmeal ....1 part

Make into a paste with water and alcohol. Make several daily applications, working it in well each time.

(e)

Mix a thin paste of flour and water, bring it to a boil and add butter or lard until the oil appears on top, cool down to lukewarm and coat the flesh side of skins with it. Let lie for twelve hours and then stretch.

Sperm, neatsfoot, kerosene oil, vaseline, butter, lard and viscol are all used in softening skins. When any oil or oily composition has been worked into a skin it should, after sufficient softness is attained, be drummed or worked in sawdust, meal or other absorbent to remove any surplus. A mild heat while working the oil in will assist the operator, hence the efficacy of the tubbing process. The warmth from the workman's body and feet together with that set up by the friction being just about sufficient. If a skin dries too much to be readily broken and stretched it should be dampened again until in proper condition. After a little experiment it is easy to determine when a skin is in the best shape for breaking up and stretching, by the way it will whiten when stretched.

CHAPTER XIII.

SMALL OR LIGHT FURS.

THE skins of animals not larger than the wolf or sheep are usually so classed, and thus would comprise about all the furs most commonly used. In dressing these we have personally had best results from using liquids No. 10 and No. 11 after thoroughly fleshing and opening up.

The length of time they should remain in cannot be exactly specified, the lower the temperature the longer it will require, and a partially spent solution will need more time than a fresh one. On taking from the tan, wash and rinse thoroughly, soak from one-half to an hour (according to the amount of grease) in gasoline, wring out, and work in heated sawdust or meal, alternately working it into the fur and beating it out until the fur is clean and dry.

The skin will not be dry yet, so hang in a dry place, in the air if possible, until the leather begins to dry out. Beam or stretch with crutch or stake knife at intervals until dry . Probably along the back, neck, etc., it will seem stiffer than elsewhere. If a good durable skin, thin down

126

these places with curriers knife, turned edge scraper or sandpaper block.

Treat the inside of skin to a coat of oil or oil dressing, say (a) or (d) and work it in by tramping, pounding or rolling, wringing and rubbing with the hands. Let it stand twelve to twenty-four hours and if soft enough, clean with sawdust, beat free of the dust and with a fur comb work out any tangles that may remain. Some claim that immersion in tanning liquids injures the fur, and undoubtedly the alum mixtures are apt to make it dull and harsh.

In case an application is made to the flesh side only of a skin it had best be washed or scoured on that side with water and soap, or soda in case acid has been used, before drying and stretching. Sawdust may be sufficient for cleaning the fur of such a skin in some cases, but for a badly scented skunk it will be entirely inadequate. The scent of furbearing animals being of an oily nature is soluble in benzine or gasoline, though not in water, so washing in either of the former liquids will remove it from furs.

The beginner should experiment on some of the smaller and at the same time less delicate skins of little value. A wild cat, or failing it one of the domestic variety, furnished a good skin for practice. It is not so difficult to dress one with snow white leather as soft as velvet. The fur of all the cat kind is prone to knot and tangle if not thoroughly cleaned, especially when it is long and silky like the lynx.

A raccoon skin may be used for a first attempt but is a little more difficult as it is apt to be more greasy, and the back of the neck at least will require a liberal thinning down.

Skins up to the fox in size are dressed either open or cased, though most of the small skins remain cased until they get into the cutter's hands.

A small beam is a necessity for working these and parts of larger skins. A piece of wood about 2x3 inches and three feet long may be tapered to a blunt point at one end, half rounded and bolted to the top of work bench or table for this purpose. All cased skins must be turned from time to time in order to work on both the leather and fur sides. A contrivance somewhat resembling a small beam with a clamp to hold the head of the skin will facilitate this in the case of minks, weasels and similar sizes.

The heads, tails and paws if preserved with these small skins need some attention, as they are all frequently made into trimming for fur sets, hats, etc. A device to answer the purpose of the stake knife in breaking up and softening small stock may be improvised by fastening a piece of steel in the jaws of a vise and drawing the skins over the edge of it. A piece of saw blade 3x5 inches or so with the upper corners taken off and ground square on the edge is about right for this.

Skins of no great value such as rabbit, squirrel or mole are sometimes brushed on the flesh side with a paste of soap and oatmeal or flour, scraping it off and oiling and rubbing afterward.

CHAPTER XIV

THE skins of bears, tigers, leopards as well as horse and cattle hides to be made up in robes, rugs, and coats may be called heavy furs, and will require considerable more labor in their preparation than those of the smaller animals. This is principally in the thinning down necessary to secure a proper degree of flexibility, as their treatment otherwise should be about the same.

These should be well reduced in thickness with the knife before putting in to tan to secure a rapid penetration by the liquor. Elk and moose wanted with the hair on are dressed in the same manner, and unless of very young animals will need to be thinned over the entire surface.

Special care should be taken not to mutilate the heads and paws of large fur skins which can be mounted as rugs. It is better to leave the final thinning of these parts to be done when they are mounted. In the case of bears, wolves and similar skins to be made into robes or garments the heads may be trimmed off before dressing, as it is not possible to make use of them or the paws

130

in such work. They may be used to repair where
such parts are wanted to be mounted for hanging
on the wall, as such decorations are quite attractive.

SKIVING BEAVER SKINS

All Except Very Thin Skins Should be Reduced in Thickness with
Curriers' or Skiving Knives.

When skins are tanned in any numbers very
little waste is allowed. The fat and grease removed from raw skins is saved and rendered or
sold, and the leather tanneries sell the cattle hair
for plasterers' use, the spent bark for packing
and fleshings and scraps for fertilizer.

It goes without saying that much more time is required for tanning ingredients to penetrate heavy skins; from three days to a week is about the usual limit. There is very little profit for the hand workman in the dressing alone of this class of skins, and the work is hard and dirty.

Cattle hides for robes or coats should be selected for a heavy coat of hair and be what are termed "spready," that is, of comparatively large area for the weight. Thick heavy skins from old animals are usually more valuable for leather making.

Polar bear skins are not to my knowledge used for any purpose but floor rugs except by the Eskimo, but they require a struggle to free them from grease. If this is not thoroughly done the white fur will turn a fine yellow and the skin itself may drop to pieces if it was allowed to stand in the grease too long before dressing.

One of the largest polar bear rugs I ever saw disintegrated in this way after it had been mounted a few years, and although it was worth several hundred dollars all attempts to repair it were useless. The hide was so crisp and tender it simply would not hold together. A sharp needle would push a piece out of it before it would penetrate.

Comparatively speaking, polar bear skins are worth less now than several centuries ago, being estimated then as a trophy of the highest bravery. Now the use of fire arms of precision has made it possible for almost any Arctic traveler to secure them, but they are still quite expensive.

Considerable gasoline is required to degrease such skins on account of their size and the heavy coat of fur. On account of the extra expense and labor involved the dressing charges are rather higher than for other skins of similar size.

We once received four irregular pieces of polar bear skin to be dressed, and on questioning the owner as to such peculiar modes of skinning, he informed us that he had purchased the pieces of four natives on the shores of Hudson's Bay. The party of four hunters had killed the bear and divided the carcass, skin and all among them. He had arrived before they separated or used any of the skin, and purchased it from the several owners. It turned out a very fair skin, and the weird design of seams made in fastening it together was hidden by the lining on one side and by the heavy white fur on the other.

Very few skins of the American Bison or buffalo will fall into the robe dresser's hands at the present time, though once so numerous. Efforts have been made to partially domesticate them, but with indifferent success. They seem essentially a creature of the wilds, unsuited even

for generous enclosed ranges. On account of the
woolly coat and the grease used by the Indian
dressers, they were an especial prey of the moth,
and with all civilized appliances would prove
difficult to clean properly. A few skins of the
muskox are handled by the trade each year, but
these never numerous seem growing scarcer too.
They are used for robes and have even longer hair
than the buffalo. Treatment similar to that for
cattle hides will fur dress either bison or musk
ox.

CHAPTER XV

SO M E species of deer being common to almost every part of America the native inhabitants made universal use of its flesh and skin as food and clothing. The early white settlers took readily to buckskin as a substitute for their coarse hand made or high priced imported cloth. In the making of men's garments for rough wear it held much the same place as the cotton ducks and drillings of today, which were not then manufactured.

By adopting the Indian mode of dressing, it could be made ready for use in a very short time, at no expense whatever but the labor and with but the rudest tools. Except in the extreme North it is but little used for clothing at the present time, but the demand for it chiefly as glove material is practically unlimited. Deer skins are frequently dressed with the hair on for use as rugs or robes, and in the far north many natives and some whites use them as clothing or bedding to repel the intense cold.

The hair of the deer family has a hollow structure more or less like that of a bird's quill, and in the case of the reindeer or caribou at least, these are partitioned off into numerous cells all filled with air. This peculiar structure makes a heavy coat of deer hair a good protection against cold and wet. The hair of the common deer is apt to be rather brittle, breaking off continually when in use. The shorter haired skins give less trouble in this respect.

The does and fawns furnish skins that dress very soft with little thinning, and are treated in about the same manner as the small fur animals. Buck deer skins are much heavier and need extensive paring to make them flexible, and after rinsing out the tan liquor and partly drying should be given at least two coats of some oil dressing. One pint of neatsfoot oil beaten up with a half pint of leached lye and applied with a brush is good to soften deer skins and light furs as well.

In the chapter on Indian Skin Dressing, buckskin making in its simplest form is described and the white man's style is but little different. Soap is commonly substituted for brain dressing and the smoking is done in a smokehouse, or lacking that a box or barrel. The skins are first unhaired, and this may be accomplished in several ways, the simplest of which is to soak in clear water till the hair slips. A tub of lukewarm water kept in a warm room will help this along.

If treated with ashes and lime the skin should be well washed or soaked in bran water to kill the lime. Some writers say that deer skins may be grained immediately on removing from the animal without soaking but I have never seen it done. Frequently it would be impossible.

When the hair and "grain" or epidermis can be readily scraped off, put the skin on the beam hair down and flesh it well, then turn it over and scrape off all hair and epidermis.

A steel tool with a square edge is best for this. A skate blade will do it nicely. If you prefer, the graining may be done before the fleshing; it is immaterial which is first.

Next dissolve a half bar of laundry soap in two gallons of warm water. While still warm put the skin in and work the suds well into it. Let it stand about twenty-four hours, take it out, wring and pull it dry. Give it a coat of oil dressing of some kind, butter or grease will do, warm the water, add another half bar of soap and put in again. After twenty-four hours more take it out and pull and stretch as it dries. A very thick skin may require a third soaking in the warm soap suds, but twice should answer for does and young bucks.

When dry and soft, skins should be smoked with a punky or dozy hardwood fire; this should give them a nice yellow tinge, much better than can be done rubbing ochre into the buckskin, as is sometimes done.

If you wish to try buckskin dressing and have no deerskin to experiment on, calf, sheep or goat skins may receive the same treatment. The humble woodchuck can be turned into a leather suitable for mittens, moccasins and other odds and ends. Buckskin vests are frequently called for as they keep the wearers warm in cold weather, repelling the wind from the vital parts of the body. For such purposes light buckskins like that from yearling deer is most suitable and should be softened by the application of more elbow than other grease. Heavy skins for moccasins should have a coat of oil or dressing applied to each side.

INDIAN MODE OF MAKING
BUCKSKIN.

Take the skin and immerse it in warm water, say two ten-quart pails full, throw in several handsfuls of wood ashes and stir well. Immerse the skin in this mixture until the hair slips off easy, then remove to your fleshing beam as before mentioned, and flesh it clean. Turn it over and scrape off the hair, using the draw knife with the handles bent straight by the blacksmith, as mentioned for sheep skins. After the hair is removed, there is left a thin skin or cuticle, brown in color. Now wash the skin in clean warm water and pass it through a wringer, such as is used for wringing clothes. Now take the brains of the animal, dry them slowly, taking care not to burn or cook them, when dry put them in a cloth and boil them until they are soft. Cool down the liquor until blood warm, then add water enough to immerse the skin in, and soak it until perfectly soft; pass it through the wringer and work it as described for the sheep pelt, until soft and dry. If you have not got the deerhead so you can procure the brains, then use lard in place of the brains and soak in this liquor six hours, then rub dry and soft, and you will have a good piece of buckskin. Smoke the skin by the white man's method.

THE WHITE MAN'S MODE OF MAKING BUCKSKIN.

Put the skin in wood ashes or lime water that is about as thick as milk or thicker, leave it there until the hair slips off easy, then put it on the fleshing beam and flesh clean, i. e., scrape off all meat and fat, after the hair is off, scrape the brown skin off also, that that lies just under the hair, (a thin cuticle skin), it is sometimes

called the grain. After this is well done, grease
the flesh side with bacon grease or butter which
ever you have at hand; then hang for a day or
two days for that matter. Now take some of the
good old home-made soft soap and make a good
suds, immerse the skin and leave it until you can
squeeze water through it with ease. Usually it
takes from four to ten days, depending on the
thickness of the skin. Keep in a warm place like
a tent, while doing this. When water passes
through the skin by squeezing easily, take it out,
rinse in clean soft water, pass it through a
wringer a few times, and work until dry. If you
have no home-made soap at hand to do this with,
use common bar soap.

Now this is fine buckskin, but when it is
wet, it dries out hard. To prevent this we (and
the Indians also) smoke it. There are many
ways to do this, but probably as simple a way as
any is to cut about a dozen switches or hard
wood about six feet long, sharpen the butts and
stick them in the ground in a circle three or four
feet in diameter, gather the tops together and tie
them, this forming a wickiup or tepee, or as some
call it, an Indian wigwam. Spread the skin on
this as for a covering, taking care to cover any
holes that are left with some other material, like
old cloth or canvas, if the skin does not suffice
(and usually it does not). Now with some dry

hardwood chips or punk (but use hardwood in any case) build a smudge inside your tepee and the smaller and cooler it is the better. The first few hours have only smoke enough to be visible to the eye, make as little heat as possible, keep in mind it is a cool smoke you want and *not heat.* Keep your smudge going until your skin is a light brown, or just a little darker than cream color, and you will have a nice piece of "buckskin." Sometimes it is advisable to turn the skin to get an even color; good buckskin makes some handy articles, such as mitts, gloves, moccasins, shirts, etc. Moccasins are fine to wear around the house, also for bed slippers and many other uses.

When a boy on the farm we used to tan squirrel skins and woodchuck skins by immersing them in water and wood ashes until the hair slipped off. Then scrape off the grain and immerse in the soft soap barrel for several days, afterwards taking them out, then washing, pulling and drying them.

We used this leather for facing for our mitts and other uses, and it was all right. The soft soap should be medium strong for this tan.

Eel skins can be tanned the same way as the chuck skins, only of course no fleshing has to be done. The skins make the strongest strings or thongs in existence.

Much "buckskin" nowadays comes mostly from a sheep's back. I will give an infallible rule by which to tell genuine "buckskin" from a deer's back. After the skin is tanned by "any old pro-ress," on the flesh side you will observe little veins or channels where they once were. They are spread like the veins on the back of the hands, only smaller; where these are found on a hide or skin, you may rest assured it is "buckskin" off a deer's back.

CHAPTER XVI.

SHEEP AND GOAT SKINS.

SUCH skins as these should be selected with care and with regard to the purpose for which they are to be used. Sheep make good coat collars and linings and may also be worked up into robes and sleeping bags. Many goat skins are handled by the trade, but the bulk of these are imported.

Those from North China are received dressed and being of heavy fur, are made up both dyed and natural in coats, capes and robes. Many thousand goat skins are received from Mexico and the Central American countries, but these are chiefly for leather purposes. The Angora goat furnishes a skin which may well be classified as fur. In fact it is often put on the market as "Iceland Fox" or "Thibet Fur" and is used for ladies' muffs, collarettes and trimmings. The skins of sheep and goats are seldom very thick and for this reason usually dress readily and soften with the use of little or no oil or grease.

To thoroughly clean the wool or fur is probably the most difficult part of the job, but the gasoline washing will accomplish this perfectly.

Repeated washings in strong soap suds and rinsing with clear water will also effect the same purpose. but not so quickly and completely. Whatever form of cleaning is employed it should be after tawing or steeping with some of the usual preparations.

For cleaning one sheep skin, dissolve a pound of soap in two quarts of boiling water and mix half of this in a tub with a gallon of cold water. Wash the skin in this until it will extract no more dirt, then use the other quart diluted in the same way to remove the rest of the dirt. Rinse thoroughly in water slightly warmed. A little laundry blue in the last rinse water will help whiten the wool. Wringing thoroughly after each wash or scouring and rinsing, especially if a roller wringer is used will help the cleaning.

It should be well shaken out from time to time as the drying proceeds and broken up and stretched as has been directed for other skins. Not being very thick but little skiving will be necessary.

If the gasoline bath is used it should be after the tawing solution has been rinsed out of the wool, and by putting in drum or tray with the hot meal it will be cleaned in short order. The gasoline will remove the objectionable mutton or goat odor from skins.

Angora skins with fleece tangled or matted

with burrs and chaff are often useless as furs.
A short or medium length of fleece is to be preferred in both sheep and angora skins. A very
heavy fleece with a thin skin is not desirable.
Sheep skins with long fleece may be dressed and
made up as wool dusters at a profit sometimes.
In order to make them attractive for this purpose
and also as rugs they may be dyed a variety of
bright colors.

For use as white furs they will need bleaching if after cleaning they still have a yellow
tinge. To accomplish this procure or make a box,
large enough so a sheep skin may be spread to
full extent on one side of it. It will accommo-
date from two to five skins, according to shape.
On the inside tack the skins, flesh side next to
the wood so they will not hang down in the middle or elsewhere. Now put a sulphur candle in
the middle of the bottom of the box, light and
close the lid. If the candles are not to be had
put a half pound of sulphur in a tin plate and
drop some hot coals or red hot metal on it to
light it. Any holes or cracks in the box should
be calked up and the lid made to fit tight before
using, but some fumes will escape anyway, so
the job had best be done out of doors. In six or
eight hours the fumes will have bleached the wool
and the skins may be hung in the open air to
free them from the smell.

When dressing sheep without the wool for leather or "imitation" buckskin, if the wool is of a good length it can be saved and sold. Sometimes it is sheared off and the skin then soaked in the lime and ashes solution, but more generally the skin is soaked in such a way as not to foul the wool, which is then pulled. To do this the skins are first wet and then painted on the flesh sides with a batter of lime, ashes and water. Placed flesh sides together, they are piled and left several days in a warm room until the wool pulls readily. After pulling the skins are to be grained and treated about as buckskin. Shearlings and skins from which the wool has been cut are shown no especial consideration but soaked and grained as usual.

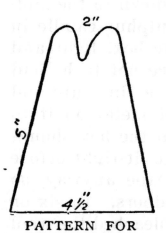

PATTERN FOR
WOOL DUSTER

As wool is of a different nature from fur it is not especially difficult to dye, and the ordinary package dyes for *wool* will do good work on sheepskins. For carriage and auto robes sheepskins are trimmed square and if it is wished to make a few dusters, cut a long fleeced skin into triangular pieces like the cut. Sew the sides of this pattern together including the rounded end, and stuff about one-half the length with wool combings or rags to shape the duster and prevent the handle marring the furniture. The handles may be made for a few cents each on a lathe of soft wood and any design to suit. They may be stained or given a coat or two of enamel paint and when inserted in the duster are held by tacking securely. A strip of colored leather tacked around will conceal the fastening and give it a finish. Comb the wool out nicely and you will have a duster suitable to use on the finest furniture or pianos.

A practical man gives the following suggestions for

TANNING SHEEPSKINS.

Many times one has a nice sheep pelt which one would like to convert into a rug; or several which he would like to do likewise with. A robe, or mittens, for mind you a lamb skin makes good mits. What we want is good results at low cost.

Like all tanning there are plenty of methods. For tanning sheep skin, the following I like best of all. First trim off all ragged pieces, then soak in *cold water* until the skin is soft, or until you feel no hard spots in it. If the skin is soft and a hard spot remains, then soak the hard spot; usually twenty-four hours is about right for the average skin. Remove the hide, place over a half round block, peeled slab or log, flesh side up, and with an old draw knife scrape off all flesh and fat. Now mix with your soft soap. A strong soap suds as warm as you can bear your hand in, and wash the skin clean, wool and all. A washboard will help matters. Also pick out all burs, etc., and make the skin nice and clean. Now you are ready for the tanning.

While the skins are damp, mix together one pound pulverized alum, half a pound saltpetre and twice the bulk of the whole mess of bran. Spread this evenly over the skins one-fourth inch thick; now fold the skin, wool side out, and let me in a *cool* place several days, the longer the better. as long as the place is cool; say a week. Now scrape off the mixture, dry out the skins and work until soft. Now a word about working soft: The easiest way, if the skin is large enough, is to take a smooth sharp edge board, nail it to a beam or tree, supporting the outside end with an upright, and with a person holding each end draw bark and forth across the edge of the board until the skin is *dry* and *soft*. Let the skin dry a while then rub a while. If this is not carried out, your skin will look like an old battered kerosene can. If your skin does not come out to suit you, it can always be tanned over again by this process.

With a heavy leathered skin, I have known the process to begin by pounding the skin with a club. I know of a moose hide that was broken this way, and by constant use was as soft as silk. In the case of fur skins, rub them in your hands, and a dry washboard will help. I forgot to add that after washing the skin in the soap suds, rinse in warm soft water and if the skin is small enough, run it through a wringer.

The treatment for goat skins is practically the same as for sheep in dressing and cleaning. The pelts (except Angoras) being more on the order of hair than wool, fur dying methods should be used to color them.

CHAPTER XVII.

MISCELLANEOUS SKINS, GATOR, SNAKE, BIRDS, ETC.

IN the preparation of alligator hides they are first soaked from two to six days, according to condition and size, the larger ones longest. After sufficient soaking they are removed to a lime solution, weaker than that used for unhairing, in which they remain from eight to fifteen days, depending on size and temperature. During this time the hides are daily or frequently removed to a stronger solution of lime. From the lime soak they go to the beam for fleshing and then to the bran drench or "bate" to remove the lime from the skin.

This bate is prepared by pouring hot water upon bran and the skins kept in this liquid at about seventy degrees, when fermentation soon begins. In this the skins are moved about frequently for a day or more, then well rinsed in clear water and put to tan in a weak extract of oak bark, sumac or gambia. This is strengthened every few days for perhaps three weeks when the hides are removed and partially dried so they may be shaved again on the flesh side to reduce the thickness still further. They are then returned to the tan liquor for several days longer, strengthening the liquid from time to time. The tanning finished, they are scoured or washed well, stretched and nailed on boards or frames and dried.

If intended for shoes the leather is now well filled with a tallow and oil dressing which is omitted otherwise, and the hides staked to make them soft and pliable. This is the commercial tanning and dressing of alligator skins, and it produces a yellowish brown leather which is also dyed black and various colors for ornamental use.

The different tawing solutions will preserve alligator skins, but will not produce the fine leather that solutions of tannic acid do, and of course it is out of the question to oil dress them as in the case of buckskin.

Sharks, rays and all the cartilaginous fishes possess skins that are very durable. Formerly many of t h e s e skins were used for polishing and smoothing wood, ivory, etc., but the g r e a t improvements in preparing sand-papers and compositions of emery have super-

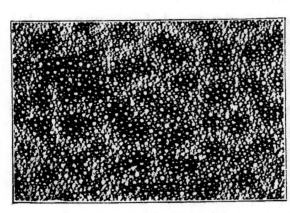

SKIN OF MOTTLED SHARK

seded them for such purposes. Some parts of these skins are very rough and hard, so durable as to outwear many sheets of sandpaper of the same size. Unlike the skins of mammals they seem to be non-porous and so proof against the absorption of water.

In preparation for use by cabinet-makers shark skins are merely cleaned by soaking and fleshing and not tanned at all.

To prepare them as leather the skins may be soaked, limed, bran drenched, scoured, fleshed and finally soaked in an alum solution (No. 1 Alum Tawing Solution) for two or three days, then removed and dried. Such skins are used principally to cover jewel boxes, cardcases and especially sword grips, for which its rough surface particularly fits it. But few such skins are prepared in this country, though in Europe and Asia many are used.

Fish skins are chiefly used for ornamental purposes such as covering small cases, boxes, picture frames, etc., but have been made into serviceable shoes and gloves. The natives of Alaska and Siberia preserve skins of salmon, cod and other fish for use as garments and bags. They remove the scales, dry the skins and work them soft by scraping. The finished product resembling kid in appearance and softness, is frequently dyed red, yellow, blue or brown and sewn together with a thread also of fish skin. Many of these garments of ornate appearance are in the museums of this country.

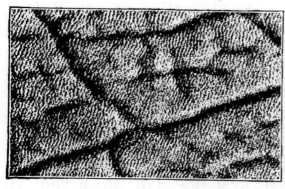

WALRUS LEATHER

Walrus hides are so excessively thick and heavy that it is out of the question to work them except in regular tanneries. The largest sides weigh 180 to 200 pounds each and are 1½ to 2 inches thick. They are used almost altogether for metal polishing or buffing wheels and sell for from 30 cents to $1.25 per pound by the side for that purpose.

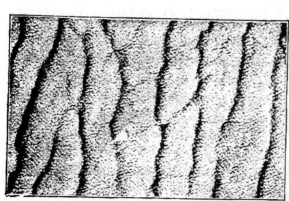

SEA-LION LEATHER

Heavy sea lion hides can be used in the same way; the light ones are prepared like seal leather. All the fur seals and some of the hair seal skins are dressed about as other fur skins are. The greatest change in their appearance being due to the dyeing process.

The hair seal leather on account of its attractive grain is in great demand for pocket books, bags and similar uses. Much of it is used for shoe uppers. In tanning the process is very

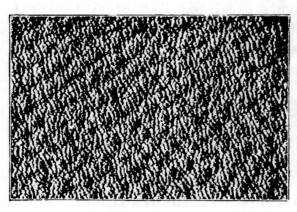

SEAL LEATHER

much the same as for alligator leather after the unhairing. Dyeing and in some cases an enamel or "patent" finish is given it. The hair seal skins dressed in the fur are mostly of very young animals, less than fifteen days old, known as "wool seals" and forming but a small percentage of the 650,000 skins constituting the approximate annual catch in the North Atlantic around Newfoundland. The rest are manufactured into leather.

Skins of the Atlantic porpoise are treated much the same as cow hides in making leather, it being necessary to reduce their thickness by splitting. It makes remarkably "easy" shoes owing to its tractibility or stretching qualities, also outlasting several pairs of calf skin shoes. The price of the green "sides" is about $2.00 each and when tanned $10 or $12.

The skin of the beluga or white whale known as "porpoise" leather is much stronger and more durable than bona fide porpoise, and on account of its size is particularly adapted to making machine belts. A single skin has furnished a continuous piece eighteen inches wide and sixty feet long.

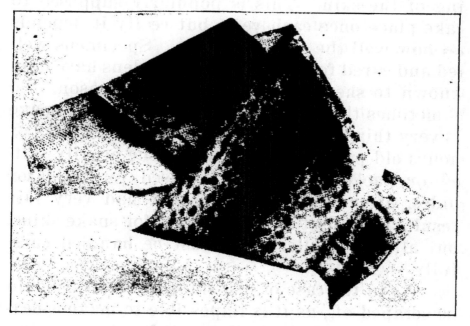

SKIN OF WATER SNAKE

The skins of frogs and toads possess a delicate grain but are little used in America. A few factories in France pay especial attention to tanning raw skins from Africa, Brazil and other tropical countries.

Snake skins are sometimes made into leather for bags, cardcases and such small articles, but the largest demand is probably for dressing and manufacturing souvenirs and trophies. They are rather difficult and uncertain in working, varying in thickness and substance, according to the length of time since the last shedding or sloughing of the skin. This is popularly supposed to take place once each year, but really it depends on how well the snake is living. Specimens well fed and cared for at Zoological Gardens have been known to shed several times in one season. So sometimes the skin of a very large and old snake is very thin and papery, being but a few days or hours old perhaps. They should be heavily salted or packed in salt as advised for alligator hides, after skinning. We have had very fair results in using the oxalic pickle for snake skins, but all the smaller ones must be handled carefully.

As in the case of fish skins the scales should be scraped off, as it is impossible to make a flexible leather and retain them. After tanning and softening them, the scale side is polished with smooth but not hot irons and sometimes rubbed with a weak solution of gum arabic or white shellac, say 1½ ounces gum to a pint of water or the same amount of shellac in a pint of alcohol. The skins of rattlers, water and other small snakes are frequently wanted made into belts, hat bands, and other useful (?) and ornamental articles by vacationists.

For these purposes they should be mounted or cemented on a backing of more durable lea-

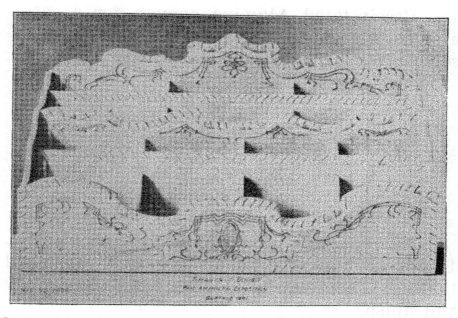

LETTER BOX, MOUNTED WITH SHARK SKIN, GARFISH SKIN, AND MOTHER-OF-PEARL

ther. A mode of tanning used in France but which we have never tested is as follows: Soak at least ten days in water containing enough sulphate of zinc to prevent putrifaction. Flesh, scrape, wash and put in

BATH NO. 1.

100 parts .... Water
10 parts .... Boracic Acid
2½ parts .... Tartaric Acid
1 part .... Borax

Precipitated Alumina enough for a saturated solution, or as much as the liquid will dissolve. After twenty-four hours transfer to

BATH NO. 2

100 parts .... Water
5 parts .... Glycerine
2½ parts.. Benzoate of Aluminum
2½ parts...... Prosphate of Zinc
2 parts .... Alcohol

Leave in this twenty-four hours then to No. 1, continue this program for five or six days until tanning is completed, then dry out, stake lightly and finish.

Bird skins are usually cleaned of flesh and fat after dampening the skin only and a preservative applied as a paste or powder. When this has had time to act the entire skin, feathers and all, is given a gasoline bath and dried out with sawdust or in the case of white feathers, meal, farina flour or even gypsum.

Swan or duck skins wanted in the down should have the stiff feathers plucked out before the tanning. This plucking must be done carefuly by hand. To free from rust or gypsum, beat gingerly and hold in a blast of compressed air such as is used to inflate tires.

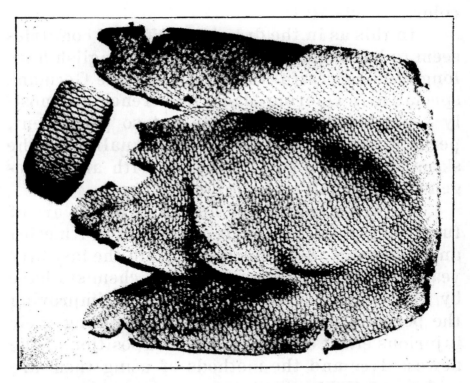

SKIN OF BEAVER TAIL AND JEWEL BOX COVERED
THEREWITH

CHAPTER XVIII.

THE dyeing of fur skins is an ancient art, but the present generation has brought it to such a state of perfection that, in many cases no one but an expert can tell when skins have been touched to deepen or change their color.

In this as in the dressing, different countries seem to have their specialties. The English have long been successful in seal dyeing, the Germans specialize in coloring black, the French use mostly vegetable dyes which are not so permanent, perhaps, but do not reduce the quality of the skins so much. The Chinaman with all his ingenuity is usually a poor dyer of furs.

Notwithstanding the antiquity of the art of fur dyeing, its principal development, in America and Europe at least, has been within the last fifty years. Skilled and conscientious chemists have by experiment succeeded in greatly improving the permanency of the dyes and lessening their injurious effect on skins. The composition of the newest dyes and the methods of using them are seldom available.

160

The number of successful fur dyers is comparatively small, and as their prosperity depends to a considerable extent on lack of competition they are not publishing what is frequently the result of long and costly experiments.

Confronted with the condition of a decreasing supply and an increasing demand, the fur trade has sought to prevent high prices, by popularizing the use of furs which were formerly considered of little value. A large part of this work devolves on the dressers and dyers who can render stiff pelts more supple and change the color of the fur to resemble that of others animals. When the dressers and dyers produced a clipped and dyed muskrat skin that resembled sealskin almost perfectly it was found that it would not sell under its real name, because it was a common fur, used largely by the poorer classes. Consequently a name was invented for it and this popular fur is now sold as "Hudson Bay seal." The fur of the conev or rabbit, a very cheap and common animal in France, is the raw material for producing "electric sealskin," "clipped seal," and "Baltic seal." Raccoon, when first introduced, was cheap and in little demand, but when given the name "Alaska bear" and "silver bear" it immediately came into favor. Skunk, which is an excellent natural black fur, though beautiful and durable, could not be sold as skunk, but as "black

RED, CROSS, SILVER FOX SKINS

Red on left, value few dollars; middle is a Cross worth three times as much as the Red; last, or skin on right, Silver, worth ten times as much as the Cross and thirty times as much as the Red. This explains why Skins are Dyed and Blended. (Photo from "Fur Buyers Guide," which explains value of these skins.)

marten" and "Alaska sable" it is in high favor and likely to remain in the class of medium and high priced furs.

Now that the prejudice against muskrat, skunk, and other cheap furs has been overcome they can be sold under their real names. Muskrat furs in the natural color are now sold as such at about the same figures as the dyed product. The pressure of increasing demand has brought into common use the fur of animals with harsh, brittle hair which are treated and sold under names which mislead the general public.

The pelts of animals such as the goat, lamb, dog, marmot, pony, opossum, raccoon, jackal, monkey, otter and others from the warmer zones of America, Asia and Africa are now worked up by dressers and dyers into quite respectable appearing furs. They are much inferior to furs from colder climates, however, lacking the close underfur, the long and silky overhair and the suppleness of leather. The dyeing also lessens their durability.

As much as thirty years ago the misnaming of furs was under the ban of the law in England and if necessary then, how much more so at the present time when two hares from the same litter may be sold at the same counter as "white fox" and "black lynx." The following is a list of some of the most common misdescriptions:

VARIETY	SOLD FOR
American Sable	Russian Sable
Fitch, dyed	Sable
Goat, dyed	Bear
Hare, dyed	Lynx or Fox
Kid	Lamb or Broadtail
Marmot, dyed	Mink, Sable
Mink, dyed	Sable
Muskrat, dyed	Mink or Sable
Muskrat, dyed and plucked,	

Seal, Hudson Bay Seal, Red River Seal

Nutria, plucked and dyed,

Seal, Hudson Bay Seal, Red River Seal

Nutria, plucked natural	Beaver, Otter
Opossum, dyed	Skunk
Opossum, sheared and dyed	Beaver
Otter, dyed and plucked	Seal
Rabbit, dyed	French Sable
Rabbit, sheared and dyed	

Seal, Electric Seal, Hudson Bay Seal, etc.

Rabbit, white	Ermine
Rabbit, white, dyed	Chinchilla
Wallaby, dyed	Skunk
White Hare	Fox
Angora	Iceland Fox
Fox, Sables, White Hairs inserted	Natural Furs

The London Chamber of Commerce has published the following list of what it sanctions as permissible descriptions:

NAME OF FUR	PERMISSIBLE DESCRIPTION
American Sable	Canadian or Real Sable
Fitch, dyed	Sable Fitch
Goat, dyed	Bear Goat
Hare, dyed	Sable Hare or Fox Hare
Kids	Karakule Kids
Marmot, dyed	Sable Marmot, Mink Marmot, or Skunk Marmot
Mink, dyed	Sable Mink
Muskrat, plucked and dyed	Seal Muskrat
Nutria, plucked and dyed	Seal Nutria
Nutria, plucked, natural,	Beaver Nutria, or Otter Nutria
Opossum, sheared and dyed	Beaver Opossum
Opossum, dyed	Skunk Opossum
Otter, plucked and dyed	Seal Otter
Rabbit, dyed	Sable Coney
Rabbit, sheared and dyed,	Seal Coney or Muskrat Coney
Rabbit, white	Mock Ermine
Rabbit, white, dyed	Chinchilla Coney
Wallaby, dyed	Skunk Wallaby
White Hare	Imitation Fox
Foxes, Sable, white Hairs inserted,	Pointed Fox or Sable

Reliable furriers seldom make use of such misdescriptive terms, though many of the smaller furriers are undoubtedly ignorant of the real names of their stock. The greatest offenders are probably the cheap advertisers and sellers of furs in connection with other businesses. Dyeing has a very legitimate use in obtaining those shades which have been determined by taste and fashion to be the most desirable for any particular species of fur.

The matter of natural coloration determines to a great degree the value of raw skins. In fur dyeing either the ends of the fur and hair may be tinted or the color of the entire skin may be changed. The first process, called blending, is chiefly used to make all pieces of fur used in a garment of the same color or to remedy minor defects. Some furs closely resemble choicer ones in every respect except color, and these are frequently dyed throughout with the proper shade and thus become to the casual observer almost indistinguishable from the genuine.

While dyeing may be a cheap and ready process in the treatment of low-priced furs, it becomes an art when applied to choice skins. Its perfection consists in the exact imitation of the proper color and shade, with the preservation of the glossiness of the fur, the firmness and pliability of the leather, and above all the durability of the dye.

The processes of fur dyeing are usually quite different from those in general use on textiles, principally on account of the deleterious effect of very hot liquids on tawed skins, for furs are with very few exceptions dyed after dressing.

Considerable experiment will be necessary to secure even a moderate degree of success, and it should not be necessary to caution the beginners to confine their initial efforts to pieces of fur of little value. Some knowledge of blending is a great aid in repair work, as worn and faded furs may be furbished up to a respectable appearance for their remaining years of service.

The leather of most skins dressed or tanned for furs is either white or of a light brown color, and to find furs with the leather colored either brown or black was considered prima facie evidence of dyed furs. This test is not infallible by any means, however as skins with light colored leather may have been top dyed or blended by brushing dye on the end of the fur only.

On the other hand, some natural black furs may have the leather only colored to prevent its being too conspicuous in places where the fur is thin or is likely to be brushed or blown apart. Skunk and bear are often treated so.

CHAPTER XIX.

DYEING MATERIAL AND APPLIANCES.

THE dyeing of furs is, on account of the diversity of skins and their preparation, always more or less a matter for experiment in individual cases. The dyes commonly used for dyeing whole skins were until a comparatively recent time, what are known as mordant dyes. In this process the various compounds of chrome, iron and alumina used form a deposit of oxide of the metal on the fibres and this combining with the coloring matter, forms together an insoluble colored body or fast dye.

The certain color developed, thus depends somewhat on the mordant as well as the coloring matter used. The mordanting may be done either before or after the dyeing. Some coloring matters will not dye unmordanted material, others such as the vegetable, fustic and logwoods, and some of the coaltar colors may be applied first and then fixed by treatment with a mordant.

The special fur dyes producing the best results are known as oxidation colors, called Ursols. The chief advantage in the use of these is the low temperatures at which they may be used,

OPOSSUM AND RACCOON DRESSED AND BLENDED

(1) Medium Opossum, Scalp, Trimmed Off, Dressed and Blended. (This one shows poorly; is

169

the ordinary analine and vegetable dyes being hardly permanent except they are used at a degree of heat damaging to the leather. Skins may be dyed either by immersing or dipping or by brushing the fur only with the proper solution.

Probably the most useful to the amateur, the repairer and fur worker on a small scale, are the dyes ready prepared in liquid form, which are put up in quantities of a pint and upwards. These are accompanied by full directions for their use.

The most used of vegetable dye stuffs for furs is probably logwood, either in the form of chips or the solid extract. It produces black and gray shades. Gum catechu for brown on sheep and goat skins especially. The fancy bright colors used on sheep's wool mats, etc., are to be had from the ready prepared dyes such as are used for all wool fabrics.

There are a few utensils which should be at hand, especially suitable earthen jars or dishes for the dye baths. Some of the solutions may be partly mixed in advance and combined at the time of using. Glass or earthenware jugs, jars or bottles should be used for this purpose. Scales like those used for weighing photographic chemicals as well as larger ones, and liquid measures in the form of large metal and small glass graduates will be needed for compounding dyes. A

OPOSSUM AND MUSKRAT DRESSED AND BLENDED

(1) Small Pale Opossum Dressed and Blended with Gottlieb Dyes.
(2) Small Pale Muskrat Blended Brown with Gottlieb Des. (The fur was brushed up in one spot, looks like a defect.)

171

thermometer similar to those used by the pho-tographer may be used to take the temperature of dye baths.

A number of brushes for glazing or wetting the furs, others for applying dye, known as dye-ing and striping brushes. A pair of rubber gloves will be needed if the operator is particular as to the appearance of the hands, and in all cases care should be used in handling the solu-tions, as many of them are quite poisonous. To prevent bad effects on those handling the dyed furs they should be thoroughly rinsed and in some cases drummed with absorbents to remove any loose dye material after the coloring is com-pleted.

The "fixing" or mordant materials are var-ious; diluted acetic acid, alum, cream of tartar, copper sulphate, sulphate of iron, bichlorate of potash, and acetate of lead being among them.

With the Ursol dyes are used peroxide of hydrogen and pyrogallic acid to produce the proper oxidation.

The proper amount of solution for various skins may be arrived at approximately only. To dip a skin the size of an ordinary opossum will require about a quart, a raccoon twice that, and other skins in proportion to their size. In dip-ping skins they should be entirely submerged and a dish should be provided which will allow of their being spread out flat and even.

All skins dipped in various coloring solutions must be again softened after drying. In some cases a regular retanning may be necessary. Usually a damping, staking and oiling of the leather will be sufficient, especially if the dye has been applied at a low temperature. Logwood dye requires considerable time at 100 degrees or over, while the Ursol dyes work at about 80 degrees F. This may be called, comparatively, cold dyeing, and when brushed on, the skin proper is affected little if at all by the application.

STRIP OF RACCOON FUR
Top Part Dyed Dark Brown; Central Part Natural; Lower Part Blended.

Most of the dyes manufactured for coloring textiles must be applied at a high temperature. In many cases an immersion at the boiling point for some time is necessary. This makes them inapplicable to the treatment of furs, as the skins would become partially dissolved by any such method. Sheep skins are sometimes dyed with these colors, by fastening them on boards or frames and allowing the wool alone to come in direct contact with the hot liquid. The successful dyer must be a practical chemist, at least to some extent, and we cannot pretend to go into the details of such a business in this book.

What are given here are hints to help the fur worker on a small scale, the repair man, etc. To such purposes the simplest processes and those requiring the least apparatus are best adapted. In making and altering furs, light or worn places must be cut out and replaced, unless the materials are at hand to touch up and darken them.

Furs that are becoming faded and "springy" are graded down by the buyers, though just as warm as they ever were. They know that it will be necessary to have them dyed before they are used and cut their prices to allow for it.

Especially is it desirable to be prepared to at least blend or darken the top hair when doing small jobs of custom work. This is on account of the limited number of skins you will have to select from. The contrast would be too much between the lightest and darkest of a small lot, to look well, made up together.

It sounds like an easy matter to dye a goat so as to resemble bear, or to counterfeit skunk with opossum, but it is just as easy to ruin a skin entirely or produce a color which no furred animal on land or sea ever had.   Experiment alone can determine just what results may be looked for.   Even the minerals contained in the water used in dyeing or tanning are liable to affect the results.

CHAPTER XX.

OF course a fur can be dyed some color darker than that which it naturally possesses. A few varieties are bleached to obtain lighter shades, but this is done infrequently nowadays.

There is at present a fad for blue furs in imitation of the so-called blue, or more properly sooty fox. Light gray furs and white ones blemished by a yellowish cast are used for this purpose. Almost all other colors used are some shades of brown or black. These added to the natural coloring of the furs produce a bewildering variety.

In the case of the fur seal, for instance, fashion has decided that the color shall be changed to a lustrous blackish-brown, resembling no original color whatever, in the animal kingdom.

The most desirable shades of brown are the dark brown, the reddish and golden browns. Blacks are sought for in dead and blue blacks. Beaver, otter and similar furs are sometimes

PALE RACCOON DRESSED, BLENDED DARK GROUND,
SCALP TRIMMED OFF FOR MOUNTING. (Gottlieb Dyes)
(This is same skin as shown on page 109 in the raw)

"silvered" by brushing lightly with a solution of acid or made a golden yellow by an application of peroxide of hydrogen

One firm which makes a specialty of ready prepared dyes and other preparations for furriers use, lists about thirty products for dyeing, besides prepared cleaners, bleaches, leather colors, etc. These are especially adapted to be used in a small way, with economy, as they do away with compounding and keeping chemicals which are liable to deteriorate.

BLEACHING FURS.

Make a solution of soda and water in the proportion of two ounces of soda to one quart water. Immerse in this two hours, wring and put in a bath of peroxide hydrogen and water equal parts. Leave in for ten or twelve hours, remove and dry in the sun or by gentle stove heat. Shake out and comb. If not sufficiently bleached repeat the peroxide bath, as it is the bleaching agent. If the top fur only is wanted bleached, brush it with soda water, one ounce to the quart of water. Let it lie all day and dry, then beat it out and brush with peroxide with no water added. Let lie over night and dry in the sun if possible. Beat and comb afterwards, of course.

GOLDEN BROWN ON PLUCKED FURS.

Apply a mixture of one fluid ounce of nitric acid and twice as much water to the fur only, with a brush. Use care not to apply too much at one time, do not let it penetrate to or touch the pelt or it will be burned. Use a brush of vegetable fibre. When brushed all over lay in the sun or in gentle stove heat to dry. If of an even color, sponge off the fur with clear water to remove the acid and dry again. If it should show spots when dry after one application of the acid solution, brush it again with it before washing.

To color sheep mats the bright shades they are commonly seen in, the common package dyes for sale at drug stores are sufficient, and they should have with each package directions how to apply and what mordants to use in order to make the colors fast. These as well as some appended formulas, call for a considerable degree of heat, so it may be well to keep the skin itself from much contact with the hot liquor by fastening it on boards or frames and immersing the wool only. Sheepskin is none too durable at best.

BLACK FOR SHEEPSKINS.

Boil five pounds logwood chips in one gallon water; when cooled to about 12 degrees, put the skin in and let it remain an hour or two. Remove, wash in cold water and hang up to dry until next day. Then prepare a fixing bath or mordant by boiling twelve ounces copperas, two ounces blue stone or sulphate of copper and sixteen ounces cream of tartar in one gallon of water, while this is still hot (about the same as the dye was used) put the skin in for two hours. Remove, wash in cold water and hang up to dry.

BROWN COLOR.

One pound catechu in one gallon of water and to fix, ½ pound sulphate of copper in one gallon water. If the color is not deep enough repeat the entire process. Of course the skins must be thoroughly cleaned before attempting to color them.

COLORING SHEEP SKINS. (WOOL ON).

ORANGE.

For each skin one ounce picric acid, dissolve in enough water to cover the skin.

MAGENTA.

Put ½ ounce magenta crystals in sufficient water to cover the skin. Dissolve these colors in a quart or two of boiling water and add enough more to make the required quantity. It should not be warmer than hands can be held in comfortably. Leave the skin in the solution until a good color is had, then remove and set the color by dipping in about the same amount of water, to which a pint of vinegar or alcohol has been added.

While drying shake and rub them to prevent hardening. In fact, work them much as in the softening after tawing. It is well to experiment on waste pieces of skins before going ahead with any amount, as this will give an opportunity to change the proportions of the dye.

Goat skins are treated much the same as sheep; some recommend using the mordant first in their case. A general rule seems to be that the hotter the dye the shorter immersion necessary.

The Ursols which have been mentioned before as being much used in fur dyeing, are sometimes difficult to procure. They come in a solid state and are to be dissolved in boiling water. When using them the color develops on the fur by oxidation, from treatment with peroxide of hydrogen, bichromate and permanganate of potash, etc. These are sometimes applied as a mordant before dyeing or mixed with the ursol solution. The great advantage of these materials is that with them furs may be dyed in a cold or at most tepid bath and produce fast browns and blacks of all shades. The manufacturers of the ursols give a few general directions for their use.

BLACKS AND BROWNS.

For blacks the products known as Ursol D., D. D. and D. B. are used while P. and 2 G. produces brown. P. produces a reddish brown and 2 G. a yellowish brown, D. a dead black, D. D. a blue black and D. B. a blue black with bluesh tone predominating. Combinations of these with the proper oxidizing agents will produce a great variety of shades. Hydrogen peroxide is most commonly used in combination with these dyes.

When using chromate of potash in a mordant *previous* to dyeing, hydrogen peroxide in the proportion of about ⅓ pint to each ½ ounce of ursol should be used and about three times that amount of peroxide where a chrome mordant is *not* used. A solution of chloride of lime may be substituted for the peroxide where brown shades are wanted.

In mixing ursol dyes, do as already described in coloring sheep skins, dissolve in a small quantity of boiling water then add cooler to make up the desired amount.

Some varieties of fur are very resistant to dye material, especially wiry, bristly hairs. These have to be treated with alkali compounds or "killed." Lime powder is much used for this purpose in company with other substances. After "killing" or brushing with these solutions, furs should be dried and beaten to free them from the lime dust.

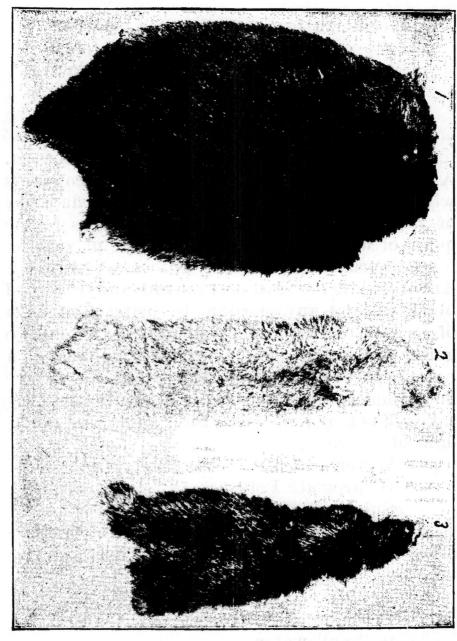

MUSKRAT DRESSED AND DYED

A common form of killing is made of

1½ oz. ....Powdered Lime
⅓ oz. .... Soda
1   oz. .... Litharge
1½ oz. .... Copperas

Dissolved in a quart of boiling water.

Add the lime last and the soda before it. Another is the same amount of lime and copperas with ¾ ounces of alum. Solutions of soda alone of varying strength, from 2 to 6 ounces to the quart of water are used for the same purpose.

Different furs require different treatment. Angora goat, for instance, is said to dye a good black without any mordant by using a solution of ⅜ oz. Ursol D. and a pint of peroxide in two gallons of water. The dye stuff should be at a temperature of 75 to 85 degrees, and a twelve hour immersion is needed. Furs will generally take a black by immersing for 12 hours in a mordant of

Water ....2 gal.
Bichromate Potash ....½ oz.
Sulphate of Copper........¼ oz.

This should be at about 75 degrees when the skins are put in, and on removal rinse and dye with

Ursol D. ....½ oz.
Peroxide of Hydrogen......⅝ pt.
in 2 gal. water.

The duration and temperature of the bath should be as before given. For merely tipping furs a much stronger solution is applied to the upper hair only with a brush. Make this solution from 4 to 8 times as strong and let skins brushed or tipped lie several hours or over night fur side together before drying. Furs like opossum and raccoon will need to be brushed with killing so the tip dye will take. In using P. and 2 G. use ammonia at the rate of ½ to ¾ fluid oz. to the gallon of water and produce the darker shades of brown by adding D. in varying amounts.

A reddish brown is secured after using the chrome mordant by applying:

P. . . . . ⅛ oz.
Peroxide of Hydrogen. . . . . . ¼ pt.
Ammonia . . . . ⅔ to ⅞ oz.
in 2 gal. water.

For darker browns use twice as much ammonia and fours times as much peroxide with ⅓ oz. each of D. and 2 G. and 1 oz. P. in the usual quantity of water. No set rules can be given by even the expert dyer or chemist, everything being dependent on the condition of the skins to be colored.

The Ursols may be made up in solution without the addition of the oxidizing agents and so kept for use or experiment, mixing small quantities as needed. It is probably best to begin with weak solutions and if dark enough shades are not produced, increase the strength or repeat the application. In many cases an interval of some time, even a week or ten days, is required to develop the full effect of the chemicals.

No fur is ever really better than a natural one. Dyeing tends to deteriorate both the hair and leather, making the former more brittle and liable to wear and shortening the life of the latter.

Furs in their natural colors will fade from long exposure to light, even when on the animal's back, and more rapidly as a dead skin. Artificial coloring can hardly be expected to be more permanent, nor is it.

OLD TI M E COLORING RECIPE.

A chapter on coloring furs would be hardly complete without directions that have appeared for years in everything on the subject. For Brown: Make a paste of equal parts powdered lime and litharge with water and apply to fur with a brush. A yellowish brown from one or two coats is darkened by each succeeding coat. Give a coat of the solution of nitrate of silver and ammonia to produce black.

¼ oz............Nitrate of Silver
4 oz........Carbonate Ammonia
1½ gi. ....Rain Water

Keep corked tight and apply with a brush for a brown. Successive coats darken.

Do not think this will be as good as regular fur dyes and at present it costs even more to make yourself, but give it for what it may be worth.

We would advise the fur worker in a small way to confine the use of fur dyes to such touch ing up and blending as is needful in combining ill assorted skins and repairing worn and faded furs.

In the recipes given, the figures are for average amounts. More is sometimes needful and less may be often used. Results are not guaranteed, nor would they be by the most expert, without a sample of the goods for examination and experiment.

CHAPTER XXI.

FURRIERS' TOOLS AND SUPPLIES.

THE appended list of furriers' tools and material may look threatening in its entirety, but it must be borne in mind that while much can be accomplished with less, it is much easier to do good work with the proper appliances. Many of these things will be already at hand, too, such as hammer, pliers, needles, scissors, etc., and considerable material suitable may be had at the dry goods stores or from the general catalog houses. Some items, of course, are only handled by the furriers supply dealers, whose price lists should be procured, as they enumerate and describe about everything needful and also keep pace with the ever changing styles.

If only minor repairs are expected with, say, an occasional skin to be made up for sportsmen as muff, collar, rug or robes, but few special tools are necessary; but if a considerable volume of even such work is to be had, quite an expenditure for tools and materials will be justified. Some things most indispensable are:

Fur Cutting Knives Awls

Fur Combs   Seal Press

Pliers   Scissors

Tweezers   Needles

Pinking Irons   Blocking and Nailing

Muff Blocks   Pins

Hammers

Furs may be cut and trimmed with almost any sharp knife but the shape of the regular fur-

FURRIER'S KNIFE

riers' knife adapts it to the purpose, and a combination of knife and comb is a particularly handy thing for the small shop or repairer.

Combs are made of steel, brass and German silver, running as fine as twenty teeth to the inch for use on fur seal up to the baby garden rakes for robe makers. There is a plyer made with especial shaped handles for stretching out the edges of dressed skins, etc., but an ordinary plyer will do. The tweezers are the usual fine pointed ones, as are also the assortment of sewing, harness and brad awls. It is well to have at least two sizes of pinking iron to suit large and small work, and the V shaped cutters will save both time and material. By cutting down the middle of a strip of felt of suitable width with these irons, two pieces of border are produced at once. Folding the felt over once expedites this job, too.

Muff blocks for stretching and shaping skins sewn up for muffs are only to be had of the supply dealers, and are needed for all but single skins made in open rug styles or with ruffled satin muff beds. The seal press is principally used when goods are sent out on approval to prevent substitution, and will not be of much use to the custom worker and repairer.

A good supply of needles for both cloth and skins is inexpensive as are the necessary pins. For nailing, long, slender brads may be substituted for pins.

Of the following supplies, it will be necessary to keep on hand a small stock of some things, like glass eyes, artificial skulls, noses, claws and fasteners. A line of samples of the various linings serve to order from, and where the skins are brought in the raw there will be sufficient time to procure them.

Lining Satin, Plain	Sheet Wadding
Lining Satin, Brocaded	Muff Beds
Quilted Lining	Glass Eyes
Rubbered Lining	Head Forms, closed
Scarf Chains	mouth
Artificial Noses	Head Forms, open
Artificial Claws	mouth
Stiffening Canvas	Fasteners, Hooks,
Robe Plush	Loops, etc.
Rug Felt	

The manufacturers or dealers will supply samples with descriptions and prices of most of these goods. The satins are usually 27 in. wide, quilted satin 24 and quilted coat lining 36 inches. Pinked felt borders are 3 in. wide, and the piece goods is either 36 or 72, usually the latter. Wadding comes in either nearly square sheets or rolls 32 and 36 inches in width.

Chains, noses, claws and the smaller head forms are sold in dozen and gross lots, the larger sized head forms suitable for rugs sell singly, and glass eyes for mounting by the pair or 10 pair lots. Muff beds have lately been handled by many large dry goods dealers at retail; supply dealers sell them in dozen and gross lots. Cloth tops or shells for both men's and women's fur lined coats are to be had ready made in a variety of sizes, qualities and materials. The addition of the fur lining and trimming completes these. New York City is the chief source of furriers' supplies for this country, and many firms there make this their business exclusively.

CHAPTER XXII.

MAKING UP FURS AND GARMENTS.

IT is not within the scope of this book to instruct in the mysteries of the fashionable furriers' work, but rather to furnish some hints to those who would like to protect themselves or their friends from cold and storm with the spoils of trap and gun.

Though the treatment of skins differs in many respects from that given cloth in making into garments, many essential points are the same. For this reason some experience in the tailoring line is useful if not absolutely necessary to the fur worker. *What we call fur garments nowadays are at most combinations of skins and textiles.*

Aside from some preparatory work, furs are dealt with much the same as a heavily napped cloth would be. Such goods, that are very good imitations of furs, are on the market. The regular shape of these piece goods, makes for economy as also the ease with which they are made up, but they will never displace the animal skins which they so cleverly counterfeit.

Unless already a pattern draughtsman, the ready made patterns will assist the fur worker as much as they do the home dressmaker. They can be had readily from the dry goods dealers or by mail at small expense, not only for coats and wraps, but for caps, muffs, collarettes and similar things. The Fall Fashion Books contain patterns of fur pieces, and quite often some are shown in the Winter Fashion Books.

In taking measurements for fur coats they should be made loose with ample allowance for winter clothing beneath. Some years ago the velvet-like close fitting seal skin coats were the style, but for real use and protection against cold, fur garments should be made loose fitting. The present generation of auto riders have realized this and are comfortable in their bulky looking wraps of coarse furs.

In cutting fur, lay the patterns on the flesh side of skin and mark it with pencil or chalk. Then with the furrier's knife (or any very sharp knife) cut just through the leather of the skin. Do all cutting from the flesh side and never try to cut fur with scissors. All sewing also should be done from the back or flesh side of furs, the necessary finishing or sewing, fastenings, linings, etc., of course are on the front or fur side.

Use good thread in sewing, for very delicate furs silk, and in all other cases linen of suitable size; carpet thread is good for medium and large size skins. Gilling thread will answer for coats and robes. Skins should be sewed with an over and over stitch, sometimes called the "Polish fur

"POLISH FUR STITCH"

stitch," and a small thread d o u b l e d is often better than a large single thread, as the latter is more apt to cut out of tender skins. A little beeswax on the thread will help it to run smoothly. Regular waxed ends may be used for heavy buckskin work like mittens and moccasins.

Thorough dressing and good sewing will turn out durable furs, and nothing is more exasperating than to have a nice looking fur gape at

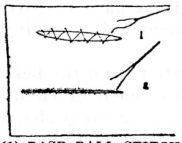

(1) BASE BALL STITCH
(2) OVER STITCH

the seams and start falling to pieces because of rotten thread or poor sewing.

In sewing a fur seam, one piece may stretch more than the other on account of being lighter leather, or for some other reason may

not look like coming out even. Now if you will take the stitches just a *little* longer on the long side it will probably be remedied; if the seam is inclined to pucker, dampen it a little and stretch, it will flatten out. Measure up before you near the end of a long seam, so there may be time to remedy anything of the sort. It is often a good plan to begin in the middle of a long seam and work each way.

The average layman knows very little about furs and is more or less at the mercy of the fur worker. Your recommendations are apt to be followed if they seem sound. As an example, a bunch of skins may come in, far from prime and in bad shape, as the coat which the owner wishes they would be a distinct failure and a poor advertisement for you. As a floor rug they might be quite satisfactory. Endeavor to show by comparison, etc., why you do not wish to make them up as the coat.

Some people seem to think if a skin is produced in the extreme north it must be of the very best. Tourists in Alaska were frequently victimized formerly and purchased at good round sums, the summer skins and shedders, culls, which the traders refused as not worth the freight. At one time a shrewd business man brought a number of raw skins of the hair seal which he had bid in at bargain (?) prices at auction, with visions of a soft, elegant coat for his wife. Were they not genuine Alaska seal skins? He had heard that the furriers could pluck the stiff hairs out and dye them to get the right effect. An army officer had a robe of some unknown but beautiful skin which he had procured in North China; could the fur be identified and valued? Inspection showed it to be trimmings from the fur shops, fox paws chiefly, and while rather unique, hardly valuable.

Repair work is a help to the would-be manufacturer, for in ripping apart old work much insight into the mode of construction is gained. Sometimes this will prove to be the easiest way to get a desired pattern.

Strive to give all work a neat finish, as lack of this spoils the effect often. Do not be discouraged by a mistake occasionally, the best workmen make them, though it is sometimes difficult for them to explain to the boss why both coat sleeves were cut for the same side. Finally, don't undertake the impossible or unprofitable. You can't imitate skunk with woodchuck, and though you may be able to pluck and dye a muskrat to imitate seal, it will be a long time before you can do it at a profit for ten or twelve cents each as the professional can.

CHAPTER XXIII.

FUR ROBES.

THE increasing use of the automobile has stimulated the production of fur robes and coats, as furs are the only material that will protect from the cold winds encountered in riding during the winter months.

Horse and cattle hides, properly dressed and lined make perfect one piece robes and are nearly wind, rain and moth proof. Select hides that are as free from blemishes as possible and of an average size. A good length and thickness of fur or hair is more important than the color, as that can be made uniform by dyeing. Such skins can hardly be dressed economically by hand in large quantities, but the large tanning concerns handle them satisfactorily at a reasonable cost.

Smaller skins make up as handsome robes, fox, raccoon, coyote and wild cat being frequently used; even selected skins of the domestic sheep look well and are as warm as any furs. Straight haired goat skins furnish most of the cheaper grade fur robes, either in the natural gray color or dyed black or brown.

197

The leather of these, especially the dyed skins, is apt to be tender, Black and brown bear make excellent robes but are not often used. Robes made of muskrat skins are used in closed vehicles but are too delicate to stand much rough usage in the open.

Skins intended for use in a robe should be

STRONG HIDE (CATTLE) LAPROBE

taken off open and stretched in the shape of a rectangle. The head skins are seldom worked up in robes, and if good may be trimmed off and mounted for the wall or saved to supply deficiencies in other skins of the same species. The tails of wolves and foxes may be left on to ornament one side or both ends of a robe.

Sizes of robes vary according to the skins used, but they are usually either 48, 54, or 60 inches wide and 60, 66, 72 or 84 inches long. The approximate number of skins of different animals needed for a robe are:

Horse or Cow 1
Kip (yearlings) or Bear.............. 2 to 3
Calf, Goat, Sheep .... 4 to 8
Dog, Coyote, Wolf .... 6 to 10
Wild Cat ....12 to 15
Raccoon, Fox ....12 to 20
Woodchuck, Opossum, Muskrat.......20 to 30

The general effect will be better if all the skins used in a robe are of about the same size.

COYOTE LAPROBE, 8 SKINS
Note tails in center.

After dressing, all cuts and holes in the skins should be s e w n up, and after dampen i n g the flesh s i d e s, stretch and tack them out flat, fur side down. In doing this get them spread as evenly as you can, so they will waste as little as p o s s i b l e in trimming.

For this nailing out skins, a number of light boards are cleated together and laid on a pair of trestles of suitable height. Several of these portable nailing boards are handy, as they can be lifted off and set on edge at one side of the room while skins are drying. When dry the skins are cut to a uniform size. If they have a darker line down the middle of the back, take care to get it in the center of each. Rather than cut down skins too much, piece out gaps in front of and behind the legs. Cut a pattern of the size you think suits best and mark around it on the skins before cutting them.

Stout glovers needles and a substantial thread like carpet thread should be used in sewing robes and rugs, as they must withstand much rougher use than other furs. Stitches should be well drawn up though they need not be fine; strength is the main requisite as the fur conceals them,

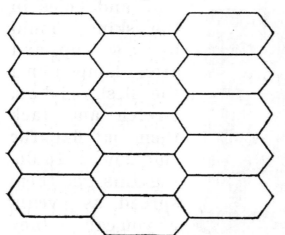

FUR ROBE OF MUSKRAT SKINS,
POINTED RUMPS

and if too close together they will, under a strain, cut off the margin. Muskrats, that have been skinned and stretched with pointed rumps may be trimmed to a point at each end and so save considerable waste. In this way the stripe is not continuous when they are put together but giving the robe a mottled appearance.

After cutting out the needed number of skins they are sewed together in rows and the rows in turn sewed to each other in the manner of making patchwork quilt. The fur is usually made to run all one way; sometimes it may be arranged to run from the center towards both sides. This sewing is all done from the back of the skins, using the regular furrier's overhand stitch.

Dampen the back of the complete robe and stretch and nail it out again to its full extent, to remove wrinkles and flatten the seams. When dry it is ready for the border and lining.

Sometimes it is necessary to turn the edge of the skin and baste it down to prevent the raw edge showing. The border, consisting of strips of felt about 3 inches wide, scalloped or pinked along one edge may be bought ready to use, or you can procure felt in the piece and cut and pink it. A small hand iron used with a hammer or mallet on the end of a hardwood block will do as good work but not as fast as a small pinking machine.

The cost of one of these is about $5.00, and where much robe and rug work is done it would be of great use, as also would a heavy fur over-stitch machine. The border may be either single or double with the upper one ¾ or an inch narrower than the lower, and usually of a contrasting color. This border is sewed on from the back, running the needle obliquely through with a short stitch on the fur side and a long one on

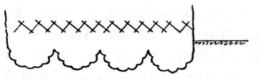

BRIAR STITCH ON LINING

the cloth. An interlining of cotton sheet wadding is to be basted to the back of the robe before the cloth lining is fastened in place. For this lining, felt is sometimes used, but plush or beaver cloth are more durable. They come in 54 and 60 inch widths, thus cutting to good advantage. All edges of this lining should be turned under and it should be sewed to the border or borders with a stitch the reverse of that used in sewing the border to the skins. That is, with a long stitch in the border, but a short one on the

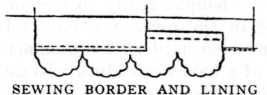

SEWING BORDER AND LINING

outside of l i n i n g. This will sink into the p i l e of the cloth, if p u l l e d snug, thus escaping both notice and wear. Of course a thread approximating the color of the cloth is used, and in sewing the border to the fur the thread used should blend with the fur, not the border.

Baby carriage robes are made of angora or lamb skins lined and trimmed with light colors, usually white, blue or pink. Quilted satin or eiderdown cloth is used to line, and wadding is unnecessary. They usually have an opening for the head and shoulders and sometimes a pocket for the feet. The sizes vary from 19x24 in. to 24x36 in.

Robes are subject to much wear and tear and calls for repairs are more frequent than orders for new work. In order to sew up rips and tears in the skins properly it is necessary to rip at least one side of the lining loose and turn the robe. Large robes, badly worn around the edges, may be cut down slightly in size if no similar material is at hand for repairs. Dress-

BABY CARRIAGE ROBE

ed, unlined goat "plates" or rugs may be bought to repair robes of that kind. Often replacing worn and soiled lining and border with new and giving the fur a good beating and combing will make a shabby robe practically like new.

CHAPTER XXIV

FUR RUGS, WITH AND WITHOUT MOUNTED HEADS.

ALMOST all fur skins except some few of the most expensive varieties are used for floor rugs and some species like the Polar and Grizzly Bears, Tiger, Jaguar, Puma, Lion and Leopard are used for little else.

A skin intended for a rug should be taken off "open," taking special care to remove the whole of the skin around ears, eyes, nose and mouth. The paws of such animals as bears, tigers, and pumas should be skinned to the last joint of the toes before cutting off, as the paws with claws attached add to the appearance of such large skins. The paws are frequently preserved on smaller skins like fox and wild cat but are hardly worth the trouble, being so small that a careless step will crush them.

Stretch the skins to dry in the approximate shape of the finished rug, and avoid drawing it out in ragged points. When sufficiently dry fold fur side in and pack or ship to the tanner. If convenient to dress it at once or put it in the pickle tub until a leisure day, the stretching and drying can be omitted.

If to be mounted with the natural teeth, clean the skull roughly of brains and flesh and dry it out thoroughly, then attach it securely to the skin; inside if it is folded up. Dress rug skins as you would any fur skin, though they will last as well if not thinned too much. The

NATURAL SKULLS—DOG WOLF, SHE WOLF, BAY LYNX, OTTER, MINK

hand scraper and small knife should be used around the head and feet.

Floor rugs made up in the flat, that is without heads, are made much the same way as lap robes; sometimes they are left in the animal shape. Cattle, sheep, goat and deer hides are often made up so, and smaller skins like raccoon and fox may be cut to a rectangular shape and joined together in rows of two to six. Sewing two of these rows together at the necks will

make a good floor rug, with the tails decorating
the ends or sides, as the case may be.

Large single skins and square rugs in the
flat, line best like fur robes, that is, a border of
pinked felt is sewed all around the rug, cotton
wadding basted in for interlining and a lining of
felt or cotton canvas sewed to the border all
around.

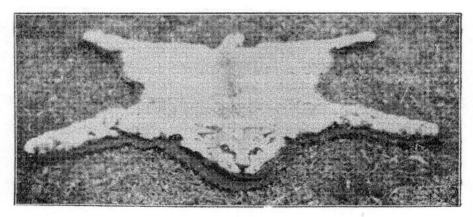

WILD CAT RUG—ONE-HALF HEAD

When heads are wanted on rugs they are
usually mounted half head or "mask" style or
full head open mouth. This half head or "mask"
mounting consists of the upper part of the head
skin only, the lower jaw is not represented at
all, and the mounted head lies much flatter to
the floor than when the full head is mounted
with the mouth open. For mounting with open
mouth either the natural or artificial teeth are

necessary. The latter may be had already placed in an artificial skull, or separately.

These open mouth head forms have the interior of the mouth and tongue modeled, and finished with paint or colored wax. Their anatomy is as nearly accurate as is necessary and practical, and examination of one will aid you if it should be necessary to model a few heads that may be wanted with the natural teeth.

The forms for half heads are so cheap that unless a certain kind is wanted in considerable numbers it is better to buy them. In case the making is undertaken, make a plaster mold of the upper part of

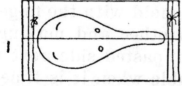

(2) MAKING MOULD FOR HEAD FORM
(1) FINISHED MOULD

the head, in two pieces, by imbedding a skinned head in clay or sand up to the mouth and pouring plaster of paris over it. Before doing this scoop out the eyes and partly fill the sockets with clay, so the paper form may have a depression in which to set the glass eyes. The plaster should be mixed with water to the consistency of thick

cream. A bottomless box of thin wood will prevent it spreading around too much, and a stout
thread stuck along the top of the head, and
pulled up through the plaster as it *begins* to
harden will cut the mould in two pieces. An ordinary cigar box without the bottom is about
right to use in getting the mould of a fox or coon
head.

To make a paper form in this mould, make
a cup of flour paste and soak a few handfuls of
building or coarse wrapping paper. The paper
should be torn in pieces approximately 3 to 8
inches square, according to the size of the head
and after soaking in water 10 or 15 minutes be
squeezed about as dry as can be with the hands.
Paste a number of pieces on one side and press
them into the inside of the mold with the fingers,
letting them overlap each other and making a
complete layer. Put the unpasted side next the
mold or there may be trouble when it is time to
remove it. Repeat this process until there is
from 5 to 10 layers of paper in place, the number
depending on the thickness of the paper and size
of the head. In order to get each layer complete
and so make the form of uniform thickness it is
best to have paper of two colors and use them in
alternate layers. Common paper flour sacks are
nice for small heads, as they are very tough paper
and being of a different color inside, the pieces

are merely reversed every other layer. Let the edges project somewhat from the mold and trim off with knife or shears after removing the form. Set the mold with its paper lining in a warm place a few hours to dry. When the paper is about dry cut the string and free the mold from the hollow paper cast.

If a mold like this is made from each species of animal received in the flesh, it will not be long until a record is on hand of the facial characteristics of most of the fur bearers, which will be extremely useful. The whole operation is not very formidable, and the forms need not be made at once; in fact, it is best to wait until several molds are on hand, as one batch of paste and paper will fill them all.

These forms are complete for mounting half-heads, and if a mould is made for the lower jaw may be fitted with the natural teeth and completed as open mouth heads. To do this successfully requires considerable practice and some natural ability for modelling.

The bones of upper and lower jaws containing the teeth should be wired to the paper forms and set firmly in place with plaster of paris to which a little liquid glue has been added. A very little glue will retard the setting enough to give plenty of time for modelling and make the plaster much harder and less likely to crumble when dry. If this plaster and glue has a quantity of ground paper pulp mixed with it, the weight and also the liability to crack will be reduced. The best finish for the inside of the mouth is made of equal parts beeswax and paraffin, colored with tube paints. Melt the wax together and dipping out a spoonful, squeeze a little color into it and stir until well mixed. Add this gradually to the rest of the wax, stirring as you do so. Cakes of wax of suitable colors for mouth finishing are carried by dealers in taxidermists' supplies.

The tongue may be either modeled in place or made separately and put in after waxing both it and the mouth. Very small tongues are often whittled out of wood. A little glue on the bottom and a finishing brad, set in and covered with a drop of wax hold them in place, and a few brushes full of hot wax connect them with the mouth. Melt modeling wax in pressed tin cups and apply with small flat and round brushes. It can be worked into shape with warm metal tools, and should not be heated too hot as that turns it dark. The above directions are given, as the owner of a skin frequently wishes the natural teeth used.

In ordering head forms from dealers, give the name of animal and the distance in inches from nose to eye and eye to ear. In an emergency, a half head form may be built up with tow or excelsior on a base of thin board, winding the material into shape with thread or cord and giving it a heavy coat of clay. Cut the board into the shape the head would have, if it were split back from the corners of the mouth. Before mounting, the skin of the head must be well pared down and stretched to its full extent around nose, eyes and lips, and the ears skinned or pocketed to their tips. Sew up all cuts and holes, dampen the head skin and give it a coating inside with arsencial solution if you wish to keep insects away. We have to omit this on fur clothing and run the chances, but rugs are not in such close contact with the owner's person.

Cover the surface of the form with modeling clay or a mixture of water, glue and whiting if you prefer. Set the glass eyes in their places. Cut two pieces of pasteboard the shape of the ears but a little smaller, and after coating both sides with glue slip them inside the ears. Now put the skin on the form, get the ears, eyes and nose in place and drive a few pins through skin and form, in a line along the center of the head. You probably pared away little bunches of muscle attached to the skin around the base of the ears, eye brows and base of the whiskers, each side of the nose. Replace them with wads of tow and clay, and mold into shape with the fingers on

the outside of the skin. Shape the nose with nostrils open and place the eyelids right, using the
point of an awl and the fingers. Draw the skin
down each side and sew around the edge of form
with coarse stitches.

Dampen and poison the whole skin on the
inside, if all holes are repaired, and laying it on
the floor or a nailing board, stretch and nail in a
line from head to tail, fur side up. Stretch the
legs as you want them and nail at short intervals
around the edge of skin.

There will probably be folds of skin between
the legs and body; fold these over and when dry
cut out and sew up gores of sufficient size to
make the skin lay perfectly flat. Do this after
the skin has dried and been removed from the
nailing board. Trim the outer edges to give it an
even outline and it is ready for border and lining.
Stuff the head form with some paper or excelsior
and sew a piece of cloth over it to keep it in
place.

If a small skin like fox or wild cat, felt may
be used for both lining and trimming; large skins
need stronger material like cotton canvas for lining. Lay it on a piece of felt and draw a mark
around it with chalk, keeping about three inches
from the skin. This cut out and pinked around
the edge makes the lining and one border. The
other border is a strip of felt about two inches

wide, pinked on one edge and sewn around the entire outer edge of the skin. Gather it neatly when rounding the head and paws. If the tail is bushy like a wolf or fox, a border or lining for it is not necessary; short furred tails should have both.

This border is sewed on as a robe border is, using good thread, of a color to blend with the fur. Any fur caught in the stitches should be picked out with an awl. The wadding interlining basted in, the lining and second border combined is sewed on. Lay the skin on this and adjust it carefully to get the margin alike all around. Pin it in several places to prevent getting it out of place while sewing.

This lining is sewed on from the back to the first border, either using colored silkatine and a briar stitch or common thread and the stitch used in lining robes. The latter of course is nearly invisible, the fancy stitch in silkatine outlines the skin on the lining.

On large skins a double felt border is sewed on and a canvas lining large enough to turn in all around sewed to it. Large skins also need to be tied to the lining in several places, as is done with bedding, to keep lining and wadding in place.

Open mouth rugs are handled about the same way, pinning the skin of the lips to the form instead of sewing. Animals like tigers and lions have prominent whiskers which must be preserved and displayed to look well. These are rooted in thick lumps of muscle, which must not be cut away or the whiskers will drop out. In order to loosen them up without this happening, criss-cross these muscles with cuts which will produce the desired effect.

When the mounted heads have thoroughly dried, cut off all projecting pins, brush the fur clean of clay or dust and give the end of the nose a thin coat of wax. With a fine brush paint hot black wax on the eyelids to connect them with the glass eyes. The lips are in the same way connected with the gums of the artificial mouth.

Black is the color needed for the nose and lips of most animals; some require brown. It usually blends gradually into the pink of the mouth. Never finish the mouth of a polar bear in pink or red, however, it is in nature a peculiar purple much like a Concord grape.

In setting the ears, bend them back along the neck usually; the head with open mouth and bared fangs is intended to express a snarl. Some head forms are now made for mounting the entire head with the mouth closed, no teeth being used, and others called shells are ready for fastening the natural teeth in. Tongues, too, in

INLAID ANIMAL RUG—TWO DIFFERENT KINDS OF FURS

several varieties and sizes may be bought ready modeled.

What are called inlaid fur rugs are made with the skin of one animal set into another of a contrasting color, such as a fox skin set in some black fur, like bear or dyed goat. This makes a pleasing variety, and sometimes a large skin that is damaged may be utilized in this way. The skin of a bear or deer with a large patch shed off or torn out in the back can be made up in good shape by setting in the skin of a coon or wild cat.

To do this, cut a pattern of the smaller skin after shaping it and mounting the head if you like. Lay this pattern on the back of the large skin, taking care to get it right side up. Mark and cut out, allowing a little for the seam all around. Sew this in on the back and then line as wanted. The common goat rugs, about 30x60 inches in size, are often used this way to mount skins of fox, coon or wildcat. No border is used on these, as the long goat hair is sufficient, and the rug is lined with a piece of canvas or denim.

Considerable repair work, especially on open mouthed heads, is often called for. Broken teeth can be duplicated by carving bone or block celluloid, and plaster composition and wax will go far to repair damage.

Every fur shop should have some one capable of rug mounting, as it is something that appeals to the customer with one or two skins of a kind, who wishes to keep them as mementoes or trophies. No unusual investments in tools or materials are needed to execute this work, and when finished it combines use and ornament.

Sometimes a rug will be brought in which may possess a good head but be damaged beyond any possibility of repair otherwise. It is a simple matter to please the owner by preserving this as a wall mount. Skins trimmed for robes and garments, and those badly damaged often furnish good head skins, and if you are equal to mounting rug heads, they can be as readily mounted for the wall. In fact, no fur store or shop seems complete without a few of them around.

To do this we must have a full head form

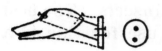

PREPARING HEAD FORM FOR WALL MOUNT

with either open or closed mouth. Put a piece of board in the back of the form and fasten temporarily with a small nail or two. Put this in the vise and adjust to your liking, then mark and saw off at the length of neck you wish. Cut an oval shaped piece of board ⅜ to an inch thick, of the proper size to fit in the neck skin at the point where it is to be cut off, and nail or screw it to the end of neck board. The head should have the nose either at right angles with the wall or pointing down somewhat. Set the neck board in head form by pouring plaster Paris around it and let it harden.

Then wind tow or excelsior on the neck with thread or cord, to the proper size, coat with soft modeling clay, and finish as in mounting rug heads. If the head is already mounted the frame and neck can be added. A hardwood panel or shield screwed to the base of the neck completes the work.

We have more than once rejoiced the owner of a rug which had been partially destroyed, but was valued for associations, by treating the head in some such way as above described.

Fur robes and floor rugs, especially the latter which are handled but little, should be poisoned on the inside, before lining, as it will greatly reduce the danger of damage by insects. The best preparation we have found to use for this is a solution of white arsenic.

ARSENICAL SOLUTION.

Arsenic (Crystals or Powdered) . 1 lb.
Bicarbonate of Soda............½ lb.
Water ....5 pts.

Put in an old dish, at least twice as large as necessary to contain the ingredients, and boil until the arsenic and soda have dissolved. Stir frequently while boiling. When cool put in a bottle or jar and label plainly as (Poison!).

To apply, dampen the skin or skins slightly on the flesh side and after mixing some of the solution with whiting to the consistency of thin cream paint it over the flesh side with a brush. It will penetrate the skin and the ends of the hairs where they enter the epidermis, favorite pasture for moth larvae and bacon beetles.

Large mounted game heads are poisoned on the outside by spraying with the solution diluted with about twice its bulk of water. Test it on a black feather and if a gray deposit is left on drying, dilute until this is prevented. Apply with an atomizer or small garden sprayer.

CHAPTER XXV.

TRIMMINGS AND NATURAL HEADS AND TAILS.

OF the making of fur trimmings, like books, there seems to be no end. Continually changing styles call for something new in this line every season. In the great fur centres prosperous firms deal in artificial heads or heads and tails alone. Thousands of trimming heads are sold every year, and many, many tails which grew several on the same animal.

The best ornamental heads are made with the natural head skins as a basis. These have the ears attached and the fur is of the proper length and disposition to look the best. The majority of them are wanted in rather smaller size than the natural head and are cut down before mounting.

Artificial skulls of paper, cork, rubber and composition are for sale in a variety of shapes and ranging in size from the smallest ermine to about ⅔ the natural size of a fox. Some have closed mouths, others show a tongue and teeth and the fad some seasons ago was for heads with movable jaws closed with springs. Noses are ready modeled on skulls, for skins minus these

220

appendages or they may be had separately to use where needed, as they always are where the heads are artificial out and out and made up from mere scraps of fur.

The mode of mounting, say a fox head, for use on a boa is about as follows: The head skin is dampened on the inside and all edges straight.

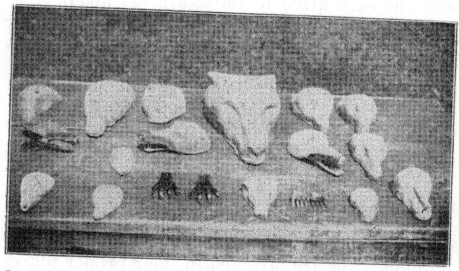

CORNER OF WORK BENCH, HORN CLAWS, ARTIFICIAL
HEADS OF PAPER AND COMPOSITION

ened out, the nose also, usually much wrinkled and shrunken, is dampened and the nostrils shaped. As it is now the skin is at least an inch and a half too long for the skull. It is flattened out and a V shaped strip about one inch and a quarter wide cut out. The point of this V is just back of the nose and the extensions of it run about to the corners of the mouth. Cutting this out removes the eye holes and separates a piece of skin with the nose and whiskers attached from the rest of the skin. This we replace and sew on, shortening the face skin by the width of the V cut out and the seam made in sewing.

Any cuts or tears in the skin are sewn up and the skin fitted to the skull. If about right this is given a coat of liquid glue on the upper surface and the skin adjusted over it. Glass eyes

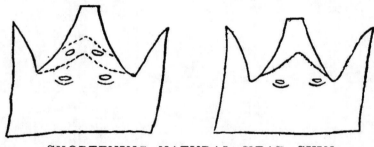

SHORTENING NATURAL HEAD SKIN

on long wires are fastened in their proper places by running the wires through holes in the head form and twisting them together inside with pliers. The inside of the form is filled with a bunch of cotton wadding and skin drawn in place under that of the upper lips, fastening it by pins and sewing.

The ears are adjusted and sewed and pinned in place. If it looks about right now, the head may be set to one side to dry, wrapping it with tape or strips of cloth first if it seems disposed to get out of shape. When dry remove the wrappings and all unnecessary stitches and pins, and touch up the lips and end of nose with black varnish.

If the natural ears are too large in their full size, cut out the base, using the tips only. Where the natural ears are missing or too badly damaged to use, bits of skin with short fur from the paws may be made to do duty for ears by clever shaping. When the heads are made from waste bits of fur it will probably be necessary to clip it about the nose.

A head clamp is on the market whereby it is possible to make fur heads quickly and perfectly and with which but little skill is required to make most artistic heads. Heads can be made with rubber skulls or without, the result in either case being a well shaped head.

In using this contrivance the skin is sewed up as usual, dampened and drawn over the head form and placed in the clamp, where it is left until dry. On removal the shape is retained permanently. Shaping by hand is done away with and the heads made in this way are uniform in shape and general appearance. It is made in three sizes suited to the following skins: Small, mink, ermine; Medium, sable, marten; Large, fox, lynx and fisher. Paws of the smaller fur bearers are used in large numbers as trimmings, chiefly the natural paws complete, on the best grade of work. When cut from the skins, they should be carefully cleaned with hand scraper, etc., and if the natural claws are attached so much the better. Artificial claws are made in horn, pyroline, glass and metal which will take the place of those missing.

Tails are a most important part of most fur skins, and the loss of a tail from such skins as should possess a beautiful fluffy brush cuts its value sharply. A black or silver fox skin without a tail would be like Hamlet without the Prince of Denmark. Still many are destroyed and many are wanted, where tails never grew, so the furrier is called on to supply them. The best artificial tails are made of strips of long haired fur sewed spirally on a core of cord or similar material. Machines produce the cheaper grade of artificial tails.

Fur band trimming is used in great variety in both dyed and natural furs. This is made of furs cut and sewn in long strips, varying in width from ½ to 2 or 3 inches. The plucked and dressed skins of swans are mostly used in this way. Band trimming is made up both length-wise and crosswise of the fur, probably more the latter way, though. Buttons, frogs and loops covered with fur are required for garment fast-euers, etc.

CHAPTER XXVI.

COLLARS, CUFFS, AND ODD PIECES.

A FEW skins can be worked up to good advantage as collars and cuffs to smarten up an old coat. The best way is to cut a paper pattern from the garment, allowing for seams and thickness of the fur. Some furriers make a detachable fur collar which may be worn with any overcoat. It requires 1 wild cat or otter, 2 raccoons, or 5 or 6 muskrat or skunk skins to make, and is cloth lined. The auto hood for ladies protects the ears and head from cold wind, and is made of about the same amount of fur. Cut on the pattern of a cloth hood, with a deep fur facing in front.

Hand bags and purses are little novelties that can be made up from scraps of almost any of the short haired furs. Plucked otter and beaver, ocelot and leopard skins are good ones to use in this way. The larger bags will need a lining of chamois leather or buckskin. An old leather purse or bag will furnish a suitable pattern. Very small fur heads, the size of ermines, can be used to ornament fur purses. At one time numbers of alligator paws were made into purses

225

for tourists in the Southern states. These are usually without metal mountings, being simply of leather.

To make them the skin of the alligator foot was removed entire by cutting around above the 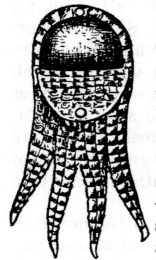 wrist and turning inside out nearly to the end of the toes. The toes were disconnected at the last joint and the nails left with the skin. When this had been duly dressed, the toes were slightly stuffed with cotton or tow to keep their shape, and the skin of the wrist cut in the shape of a flap to close the purse. A strip of "gator" leather folded and stitched made a suitable

ALLIGATOR PAW handle, and the addition of a
PURSE chamois or velvet lining completed a unique souvenir. The killer of a good sized 'gator would acquire the material for four novel purses besides sufficient leather for more than one bag and other small articles like belts and match safes.

These latter articles are often made from the dressed skin of snakes also. While not furrier work by any means it is often difficult to find any one to make them up, and the skin dresser may capture a few stray dollars in this way.

Alligator leather is quite strong but snake skins, unless of some of the very large tropical species, will require to be backed with something substantial. A stout strip of calf skin is necessary to make a belt, lighter leather is sufficient backing for snake skins, made up as hat-bands, match safes, purses, and small bags.

Dampen the dressed snake skin and then cement it to the backing with a cement which

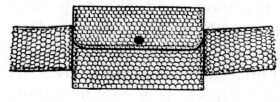

may be procured at leather stores. The backing should be cut of the exact size wanted and the snake leather enough larger to be turned well over the edge of the same all around. This

SNAKE SKIN BELT PURSE AND SECTION OF BELT

margin should be wide enough to receive a row of stitching, which may be done with an ordinary sewing machine in most cases. This leather stitching, of course, is on the face of the work and should be done with a double thread as a harness maker does.

The match case shown is from a single piece of alligator 6½ or 7 inches long and 2 wide, folded and stitched together. A piece of emery paper is glued on the front. Snake skin backed

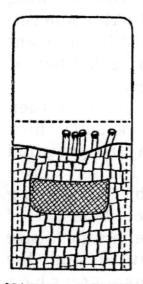

with thin leather may be used for the same thing, but it should be stitched around flap and all.

The belt purse is made in much the same way, of one piece 4 inches wide and 5 or 6 long. The belt is run through loops in the back and the flap fastened with a button or glove fastener. It is used for car tickets, cards, matches, etc. Of course these sizes can be varied to suit the case. Snake skins work up to the best advantage in such things as these on account of their shape.

MATCH HOLDER
Alligator Leather

The other small article shown is a tobacco pouch which is of buckskin or something similar. The two side pieces about 6 inches long and a strip 7 inches long and 1½ wide is cut into fringe. This

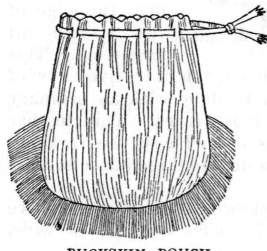

BUCKSKIN POUCH

is sewed in when the other pieces are sewed together inside out.   Turn it right side out and run a thong through the slits at the top and it is finished unless you wish to try your hand at bead work, or embroidery on the sides.

It has been said that no white man or woman either can make a good buckskin shirt, and perhaps it is so; we don't see many of them worn nowadays.   However, if any one wants to try it here is the device of a man who has made and worn

BUCKSKIN SHIRTS, A. F. WALLACE

Here again, for a pattern it is best to take a comfortable fitting shirt, rip it apart, dampen it and press flat, then cut out your pattern.   As for the gloves, sew inside out, and turn, but be very careful and have plenty of room across the shoulders and chest.   It seems that a buckskin shirt needs more room here than any other kind. If you want the fringe, then cut a piece about two and a half or three inches wide, cut the fringe one and a half or two inches deep, and sew into the shoulder seam down to the wrist.   Use a three cornered needle or a "buckskin needle," so called for this work, and the linen carpet thread.

With a knit jacket and the above shirt, you can stand some cold.   Do not have it open in front, like a common shirt, but leave one shoulder seam open from the neck to the top of the shoulder, and have it button or lace.

Buckskin if properly smoked, can be washed in tepid soapsuds, and dry soft. If not, rub soft and smoke as before directed.

Perhaps you are not aware of the fact that a good buckskin shirt brings from eight to ten dollars, and are scarce at that. You will need two large hides, or three small ones for the average man.

Vests are made of buckskin and sometimes of calf and colt with the hair on. These are mostly used for riding in cold weather and should be high cut to protect the chest. They are patterned after and lined much as cloth vests are. About the only place where the riding leggins or "chaps" of bear, deer or angora skin are seen now is at the Wild West shows.

Fur lined sleeping bags may be made from very cheap furs and still be desirable for the out door sleeper in cold weather. The outside bag should be of heavy canvas made in plain bag shape large enough for the user. Get this canvas in brown if you can; it will get dirty anyway when in use. Make the fur lining the same shape and nearly the same size as the outside. In this way but little strain comes on the fur, preventing it from being torn by the movements of the occupant. Sew the two bags together well at the top and tack the lining to the canvas at the bottom and sides in several places. This will tend to keep it in place, and yet permit it to be removed for repairs without ripping both bags to pieces.

For the inner bag or lining almost any kind of fur may be made use of. Use whole skins if you can; scraps and pieces are just as warm but there will be many more seams and seams are the weak point in fur construction. Pale and faded skins can be worked in these linings without coloring, they are more durable so and as warm as any. Cheap 'coon or opossum and the skins of short wooled sheep or lambs are suitable for this use.

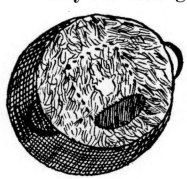

FOOT MUFF

Any one taking long rides with horse or auto in winter will appreciate a foot muff. This resembles a foot stool, in the top of which the feet can be thrust. The bottom and sides of this are usually of some stout cloth or canvas and the top of a short haired skin. In the top is a slit to which is sewed a pocket of some rough fur, large enough to contain the feet. Its shape (the muff) should be round, about 16 inches in diameter and 8 inches high.

Make a good roll of fur around the opening of the pocket, a binding of raccoon tails is good. Fill loosely with fine excelsior, tow or something similar before finally sewing up. Put the fur top with the foot pocket attached on last and sew the cloth sides to it. A mounted half head of fox, coon or wild cat in the center of the top will add a touch of ornament.

CHAPTER XXVII.

COATS AND CAPES.

IT would hardly be advisable to begin fur working by the construction of a coat unless perhaps in an emergency as a defense against the cold. It certainly would not be likely to be stylish in cut or fit. A man's fur driving or work coat could be achieved without much trouble, using either a paper pattern or better an old coat for a guide. Coarse fur or sheepskin coats made like the duck clothing so much in use nowadays should not prove a serious problem, though a lady's fine fur coat should not be undertaken unless the operator has a working knowledge of tailoring.

In making up the coarser fur garments, skins are used whole, that is, trimmed to rectangular shape, so as to preserve the back skin, with the irregularities like flanks and flippers eliminated. In this way the average muskrat skin will furnish a piece of material about 6x8 inches. All skins used in a garment should be cut to the same size, so unless of approximately the same size to begin with, considerable waste will take place. You will see in this the advantage of having quite a

233

stock of skins to select from and the correspond·
ing disadvantage of having to contrive some ar·
ticle from a small number. Enough in number
for the purpose, perhaps, but ranging in size
from small to extra large.

This would mean cutting down the largest,
and probably the best, and piecing out the less
desirable small skins. For instance, if making a
short coat that will require forty muskrat skins,
try to get fifty to select from; this will allow you
to eliminate some 10 of the extremes in size, the
largest and smallest.

When preparing skins to cut for robes or
garments in this way, sew up all damaged places
and cuts, dampen and nail. Mark the center line
of the back, and lay a pasteboard pattern of the
size fixed on, on the skin to mark around. This
pattern should be made with a square so as to
be perfectly even and marked in the center also.
Now unless there is a large numbr of skins to
select from it is not likely that they will all
match in color.

They will be just as warm but to get them
the same shade the lighter ones must be touched
up until all about correspond with those natur·
ally darkest. With an unlimited number to
choose from, they can of course be sorted into lots
of similar size and shades. This is in regard to
fur garments made in their simplest form, for

the primary purpose of furnishing warmth to the wearer.

The more elaborate fashionable furs are cut and pieced by the furriers in a way that is almost beyond belief. The most elaborate patterns are worked out in fur of different shades and lengths. Mink skins are "dropped" from 18 to 28 inches in length, or the same skin may be cut into two longitudinal strips, each 2 or 2½ inches wide, in this way producing stripes of alternate long and short, light and dark fur. Muskrat are "dropped" in the same way to resemble mink,

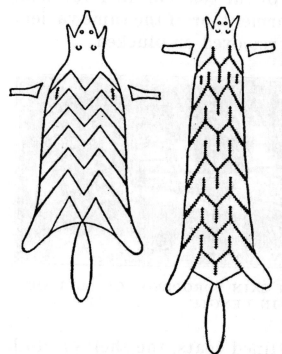

"DROPPING" FOX OR OTHER SKINS
M METHOD

and furs are frequently cut so as to make the stripes conform to the lines of the wearer. It is nothing unusual for an examination of the inside of a fur garment to show no single piece of skin much wider than a man's thumb. These very

beautiful and unique garments call for a high
degree of skill in the fur operator and command
high prices, but they are not designed for nor will
they withstand hard usage.

It is customary to make the collars and
sometimes the cuffs of fur coats of finer fur than
the balance of the garment, or of the same variety
with the long hairs removed or plucked.

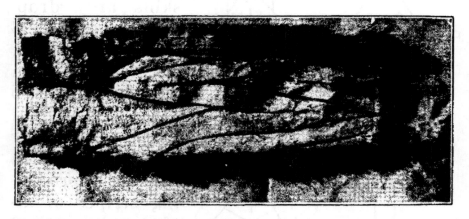

SECTION OF RACCOON SKIN "DROPPED" OR "LET OUT"
IN LENGTH

In making fur lined coats, the shell or cloth
top may be procured from the dealers, ready for
lining. They will furnish the necessary information as to measurements, and supply samples
of the cloth, usually kersey or doe skin. In these
garments the sleeves are frequently lined with
cloth. Both men's and women's heavy fur coats
may be lined with either quilted lining or wool

cloth like mackinaw. Silk and satin linings are suitable for the fine furs, and they should have an interlining of wadding to prevent undue wear from the seams in the skins.

FUR LINED COATS FOR LADIES OR MEN REQUIRE:

Kind	No. Skins
Mink	50-55
Skunk	45-50
Beaver	9-10
Muskrat	About 50
Horse or Cow	1
Calf or Colt	6-(

MEN'S AND LADIES' LONG COATS
48 TO 52 INCHES LONG

Kind	No. Skins
Horse or Cow	1 large
Kip or Pony	2- 3
Calf or Colt	6- 8
Raccoon	22-30
Wild Cat	15-20
Skunk or Opossum	25-30
Fox	20-25
Coyote	10-12
Muskrat, Mink	50-70

SHORT COATS, (ABOUT 36 INCHES)

Horse or Cow	1 medium
Calf or Colt	5-6

SHORT COATS (ABOUT 36 INCHES)—Continued

Kind	No. Skins
Raccoon	15-20
Wild Cat	10-12
Skunk or Opossum	15-20
Fox	10-12
Muskrat and Mink	40-50

The actual number of skins for a coat varies greatly on account of the size of the wearer and condition and size of skins.

Not many fur capes are made nowadays, though they were once much used by men and women both. The coachman's heavy fur cape has been replaced by the chaffeur's fur coat. At one time many evening wraps were made of fine furs with silk and satin linings. These were shaped somewhat at the shoulders, without sleeves but with slit openings for the arms, and on account of their width, required a comparatively large amount of material to make.

Accompanying this is the pattern for a fur cape. This is in a girl's size but can be enlarged to suit. It is composed of two parts for cape, four for neck band and four for collar, besides the lining, which is practically identical in shape and size with the cape.

The front edges of cape are turned under about 1½ inches to form a facing and the V shaped piece dart removed on each side, shape it to the shoulders. Skins should run from top to bottom and opossum or muskrat are very suitable to work out the design with.

Interline cape with wadding basted to the skins and use canvas stiffening in neck band and collar. These have fur on both sides, and should

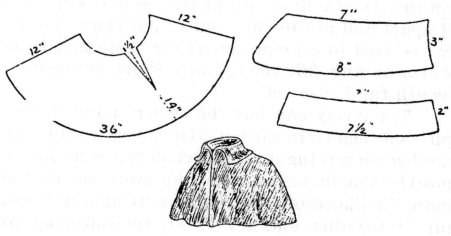

FUR CAPE AND PATTERN

be sewed up wrong side out, then turned and sewed around the neck of cape. The lining is added last.

Remember the furrier cannot make use of the tailor's hot iron for pressing goods, removing wrinkles and flattening out seams. Of course an iron may be used some times, but never hot. Dampening and stretching are used instead.

CHAPTER XXVIII.

CAPS, MITTENS AND GLOVES.

THESE are the small articles most in demand probably and are not difficult for the aspiring fur worker to produce. Two styles of cap, the army pattern and the visor and ear laps and the plain round visorless cap are oftenest made up in fur. If other styles are wanted take a cloth cap of the desired kind, rip it apart and use to cut a set of patterns. Muskrat is used to a great extent for these and is as warm as any fur, though any short or medium length fur looks well.

The Army cap has the crown made in two pieces as shown in the cut. Of course a skin may need some piecing out, but whole skins as far as posible should be used, as the more seams the more likelihood of rips. After cutting a pattern, pin it together and try it on, remembering to allow for a lining. The ear laps and visor should be of fur on both sides, so there is really eight pieces to be cut for the cap. Sew the crown together first inside out of course, sew the pieces for visor and ear laps in the same way and then turn them.

Some pieces of either common 8 oz. or stiffening duck should be cut of a size to slip inside these when turned, to help keep them in shape. Then after the crown is turned they can be sewed to it. Turn in the lower edge of crown all around so no raw edges will show.

The crown is put together with the seam running fore and aft, from the center of the visor to the back of cap. Line the cap with some

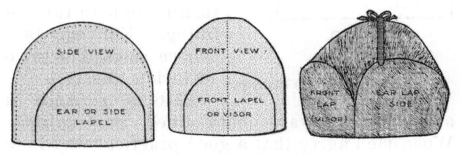

THE ARMY CAP PATTERN

wool material or better with quilted coat lining. Cut and sew up the lining in the shape of the crown or like a skull cap, and sew it in with the edges turned in. If preferred this cap may be made up with a band to turn up all around instead of the visor and ear laps. In doing this allowance should be made for the thickness of fur on the cap over which the band must go.

The round or "pill box" shape cap has only two pieces, the band and crown. The band must be the proper size to go around the forehead with allowance for the lining.

The crown piece is slightly oval and just large enough in circumference to go inside the band. Quilted lining is sewed up in the same shape, slipped up in and sewed in place at the lower edge, turning in both fur and lining. Fur ear tabs can be made and turned inside this cap.

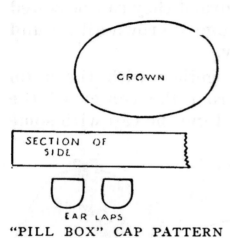

CROWN

SECTION OF SIDE

EAR LAPS

"PILL BOX" CAP PATTERN

Mittens are made in a variety of ways, both lined and unlined. Woodsmen agree that a good practical way is to make them unlined and wear a cloth or knit mitten or glove inside. This can be removed and dried out without trouble.

Made with the hair or fur inside they are quite comfortble for some purposes. Trimmings of cattle hides from robes may be utilized for such mittens as these and for driving, handling wood or fodder and similar odd jobs they are just the thing.

I. They are made of four pieces, one for the back, two for palm and one for the thumb. To get a mitten pattern lay the hand on a piece of stiff paper and mark around it. Make an allowance of ¼ to ½ inch for seams in cutting out.

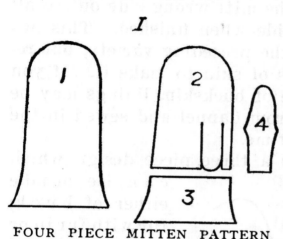

Cut and make one out of an old piece of cloth first. If it is about right go ahead with the fur ones. Sew them inside out and turn them. It is a good idea to make the wrists two or three inches long and then turn

FOUR PIECE MITTEN PATTERN

them over, making a fur roll that will fill the coat sleeve and exclude cold wind.

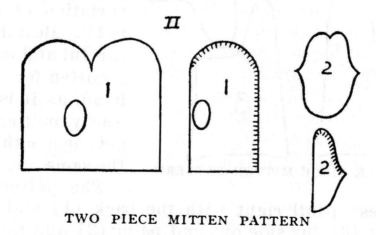

TWO PIECE MITTEN PATTERN

Something similar is the two piece mitten, II, the pattern for which is got by the same method. This way the place for the thumb hole can be determined. Make the pattern plenty large and sew up the mitt wrong side out so all seams come on inside when finished. This has fewer seams than the preceding variety, but requires larger pieces of skin to make it. If you wish to make these of buckskin, linings may be cut the same size from flannel and sewed in the seams at the same time.

Pattern III is a three piece design which can be made either of buck, fur with fur in or with palm of buck and the rest fur outside. A variation of this is IV. Be a little careful and make a mitten for each hand, as it is an easy matter to get them both cut the same.

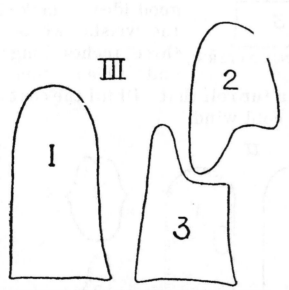

THREE PIECE MITTEN PATTERN

The pattern I makes up all right with the back (1) and the wrist (3) fur side out and palm (2) and thumb (4) of buckskin.

No specific directions can be given for glove making. To get a pattern the best plan is to rip an old pair apart, dampen them and press them flat. Use the pieces to mark out by and sew them up as for mittens. These patterns as well as those for moccasins may be made up in duck or other heavy cloth if skins are not to be had.

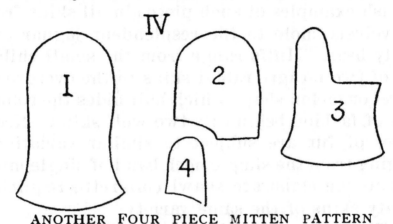

ANOTHER FOUR PIECE MITTEN PATTERN

The number of skins required to make a fur cap is:

Muskrat, medium   4
Beaver, medium   1
Raccoon, large   1
Mink, medium 4
Calf... small 1 or 2 from medium

One pair of gloves or mittens will require 6 or 8 large muskrat skins, 1 medium beaver or 1 medium otter skin. Dog and calf skins will make from 1 to 3 pairs of gloves or mittens from each skin. When making a horse or cattle hide into a robe, there are generaly enough pieces left to make a pair of mittens or gloves.

CHAPTER XXIX.

MUFFS AND NECKPIECES.

THIS form of fur wearing is perhaps the most universal, and the streets of any large city during the colder months will furnish examples of such pieces in all skins from the velvety mole to the resplendent jaguar and lordly bear. Muffs range from the small child's size of two meagre rabbit skins to the overgrown barrel or melon shape which half hides the robust lady of fashion behind its two wolf skins. Neckpieces of fur are subject to similar variations, ranging from the simple neck band of single mink skin to the elaborate shawl collarette requiring twenty skins of the same variety.

The fashionable shape of muffs is changing constantly, one of the oldest shapes being round and straight from end to end like a section of stove pipe. These are still being made, as are also the half round, pillow, rug and melon designs.

In making up furs and especially muffs and boas or collarettes from small skins a certain difficulty is apt to confront the fur worker. One skin like the mink, for instance, is not long enough to reach around the desired circumference, two would be too long, to add a few inches without spoiling the appearance is difficult, though when skins slightly dissimilar are joined at the edges it only results in a slightly striped pattern.

It seems necessary to lengthen the skins a few inches each and this is called "d r o p p ing" or "l e t t i n g out." The open skin is flattened out and marked on the inside with a number of M shaped marks. These are closest together in the w i d e s t part of the skin and they all center exactly on the dark stripe of the animal's back.

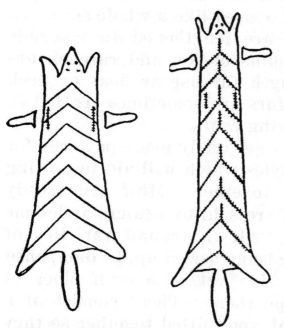

DROPPING FOX SKINS FOR BOA—
V METHOD

After cutting on these lines the skin is sewed together again and here is where the desired length is gained.

Whenever a V shaped cut is run into the skin, the point of the V is sewn up for a short distance.

This of course throws the next piece that much further down. If ten cuts were made and the points of each sewed together ½ inch a gain of nearly 5 inches in length would result. Of course this diminishes the width somewhat. When the sewing is finished the skin will be full of puckers and wrinkles, but they are removed by dampening it and nailing out flat, after which the edges are trimmed and it is used like a whole skin. In this way muskrat are lengthened to resemble mink, and single skins of fox and raccoon are given requisite length for use as boas or neck scarfs. The finer furs are sometimes treated in this way when making coats.

It is possible to get ready made patterns for muffs of various styles which will aid in cutting and putting them together. Muff beds ready lined and trimmed are sold by dealers and some dry goods houses. All the round varieties of muffs should, after being sewed up, be dampened and nailed wrong side out on a muff block of some kind to shape them. These consist of a number of pieces of wood fitted together so they may stretch the muff to its full size, something on the order of a shoe tree. Small single skins mounted on ruffled satin muff beds and as flat rug muffs need not be blocked.

By way of ornament heads and tails are used on many muffs. When large skins like fox and wolf are used a mounted head on one end of the muff and a tail at the other looks suitable. With mink which require four to eight skins there may be a row of tails across the muff or heads and tails both.

MUFF OF MINK SKIN, SHOWING METHOD OF SEWING AND PIECING

Collarettes and fur neck pieces are greatly diversified. Probably the simplest is the animal shape, made from a single large coon, fox or coyote skin. To get the proper length and width for this the skin should be "dropped" as before described, trimmed straight on the sides, the front legs cut off and the holes in the skin sewed up. After the head is mounted the skin may be sewed together wrong side out, nearly to the head and then turned.

The scarf may now be filled with a strip of wadding or not as you wish, and the front legs sewed in slits just back of the head. The opening remaining at the throat of the skin must be caught together with a few stitched on the fur side and the opening at the rump is closed the same way.

For doing this and sewing up the leg skins, use the ball cover stitch entering the needle in the flesh side of the skin, and really lacing up the opening. This stitch should always be used when it is necessary to sew furs from the outside, as it is the least likely to draw in the fur. A metal hook and chain or chocheted loop and olive for fastening will complete the piece. This is not shaped but is designed to be wound around the neck. Two skins may be used in a similar way only joining them at the necks and not mounting the heads. The hind paws and both tails hang down in front.

The above may be called neck furs straight, fur on both sides, others are straight, with the fur on one side only. Shaped collarettes may also be either fur on both sides or one only. Satins either plain or brocaded are used for linings.

For the shaped collarettes the pattern companies furnish suitable paper patterns, and the skins cut according to these are first sewed, then nailed out, trimmed and finally sewed up in the complete shape. The dissection of a few old fur pieces will give a better understanding of their manufacture than mere words can, and a short time spent in a fur shop would be better still.

Work out some sample patterns at first or better still, copy some piece of fur. Do not attempt too much, for many of the more ornate designs are the work of long experienced operators.

The number of skins needed to make either muff or neck piece varies according to the pattern.

	MUFF	NECKPIECE
Skunk	4 to 8 skins	1 to 8 skins
Raccoon	1 to 3 skins	1 to 4 skins
Opossum	4 to 8 skins	1 to 4 skins
Muskrat	4 to 8 skins	2 to 12 skins
Mink or Marten....	4 to 8 skins	1 to 12 skins
Wild Cat or Lynx..	1 to 2 skins	1 to 4 skins
Fox	1 to 2 skins	1 to 4 skins
Coyote	1 to 2 skins	1 to 2 skins
Beaver or Otter....	1 to 2 skins	1 to 3 skins

CHILDREN'S SETS

Rabbit or Muskrat...2 to 4 skins	2 skins

Muff Beds, made up and filled with down, from 28 to 32 inches in circumference and 16 to

20 inches in length are sold ready made, either with or without the silk lining and trimming. In making a circular muff the skins go around it and if not 28 inches in length they must be made so by the dropping process, or perhaps they are small enough so two of them joined together are 30 or 32 inches long. The advantage of having a few of these muff beds on hand will be readily apparent. They cost at wholesale $1.50 to $12.00 per dozen, and may be had in any desired shape.

In the process of finishing these, or other pieces of fur, the linings of silk or satin are carefully sewed to the skins, always turning all raw edges under. Silk thread and small needles are used in this stitching, which a woman's hands seem most fitted for. In fact, "fur finishing" is a business in itself which is almost entirely in the hands of women and girls.

In case it is not possible to procure a made up muff bed, muffs may be made up by the sketch herewith, using lining and wadding only. A muff this size requires two gray fox or raccoon or four muskrat skins. Sew the skins together in the flat to the proper size 16x20 inches, running round the muff. They will turn over at the ends better if four short gores are taken out of each side. Sew the end of the skins together and turn fur side out. Put wadding inside the skins one or more layers.

After the lining is sewed up, turn over and sew up at each end to form a casing for an elastic cord. Gather both ends on this cord, insert the lining and after turning the edge of skins under, sew the lining to them, taking care that the lining is gathered evenly at the ends.

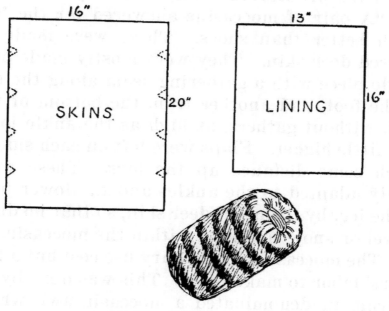

MUFF AND PATTERN

The beds ready made and trimmed are much easier to use, as they have the wadding and lining all adjusted, requiring only the addition of the fur coverings. .

CHAPTER XXX.

MOCCASINS AND PACS.

BOTH the manufacture and name of these foot coverings were adopted from the American Indians by the early white settiers. A writer describing the dress on the frontier in the pre-Revolutionary time says:

"A pair of moccasins answered for the feet much better than shoes. These were made of dressed deer skin. They were mostly made of a single piece with a gathering seam along the top of the foot, and another from the bottom of the heel, without gathers, as high as the ankle joint or a little higher. Flaps were left on each side to reach some distance up the legs. These were nicely adapted to the ankles and the lower part of the leg, by thongs of deer skin, so that no dust, gravel or snow could get within the moccasin.

The moccasins in ordinary use cost but a few hours' labor to make them. This was done by an instrument denominated a moccasin awl, which was made of the back spring of an old clasp knife. This awl with its buck-horn handle, was an appendage of every shot pouch strap, together with a roll of buckskin for mending the moccasins. This was the labor of almost every evening. They

254

were sewed together and patched with deer skin thongs, or whangs as they were commonly called.

In cold weather the moccasins were well stuffed with deer's hair or dry leaves, so as to keep the feet comfortably warm; but in wet weather it was usually said that wearing them was a 'decent way of going barefooted,' and such was the fact, owing to the spongy texture of the leather of which they were made. Owing to this defective covering of the feet, more than to any other circumstance, the greater number of our hunters were afflicted with the rheumatism in their limbs. Our women in early times went barefooted in warm weather, and in cold their feet were covered with moccasins or shoepack which would make but a sorry picture beside the slippers which at present ornament the feet of their great granddaughters."

George Catlin, the painter, on one of his trips up the Missouri, was forced by low water to leave the steamboat and set out on foot for the mouth of the Teton River, 200 miles away, with a number of half breeds and trappers. He says: "On this march we were all traveling in moccasins, which being made without any soles, according to Indian custom, had but little support for the foot underneath, and consequently soon subjected us to excruciating pain whilst walking according to the civilized mode with toes turned out. From this very painful experience I learned that man in a state of nature who walks on his naked feet *must* walk with his toes turned in, that each may perform the duties assigned to it in proportion to its size and strength, and that civilized man can walk with his toes turned out if he choose with a stiff sole under his feet, and will be content at last to put up with an acquired deformity of the big toe joint, which too many know to be a frequent and painful occurrence."

The comfort and utility of moccasins for certain purposes is unquestioned, and they are sold m)re or less the country over in a variety of makes and patterns. They seem specially Adapted to wear indoors, around camp and when canoeing. As originally)ade there were almost as many patterns as tribes, the variations being made chiefly to fit local conditions. Expert trailers were in this way often enabled to fix the identiy of unseen passers by.

The heavy oil-tanned shoe pac is used chiefly in the North by woodsmen for wear over heavy knit socks in very cold weather. When kept well oiled it is to some extent water repelling, but that is not essential as very little snow melts on the feet there in winter. They are more durable than rubber, resisting snags, etc., better, and are sold by the regular shoe trade and sporting goods dealers.

If you have some good buckskin (or other skin dressed in that way) it is not very difficult to make it up as moccasins; they will come handy to loaf around the house in or wear in a canoe, and probably you would have no trouble to give away a few pairs in ladies' sizes. If some of the old style wooden shoe lasts are to be had it is not much trouble to cut suitable patterns, but they can be made without, by a little experimenting.

The Chippewa and Sioux are two typica styles. The Eastern or Algonquin Indian moccasins resemble the Chippewa, while the Sioux are present the Plains tribes.

The Chippewa is composed of three pieces, the sole and sides in one piece, the vamp a second and a ankle or leg a third. This last was often made of heavy cloth. In sewing in the vamp gather the sides slightly and if the leather is not too heavy make the seams inside. Sew the edges of the end (a) and (b) togther and turn the flap (c) up over the seam on the outside to make the heel. Sew the tops on and dampen the whole moccasin. Keep stretched in the proper shape while drying.

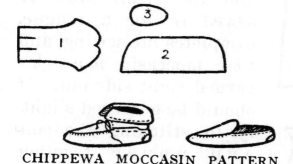

CHIPPEWA MOCCASIN PATTERN

The orthodox way to shape a new pair of moccasins is to wet them well then put them on and
walk in them until dry.

The Plains style is quite different, consisting
of three pieces also, but one, the sole, is of raw
hide or something similar. The piece of heavy
hide forming this is cut to the shape of the bottom of the foot, and in several pairs of the Indian
made article at hand, toeing in considerably. A
suitable piece of soft leather for the upper is cut

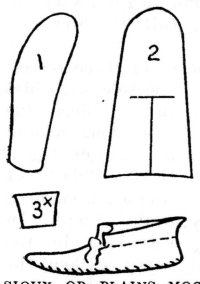

as shown herewith. This
is sewn to the upper edge
of the sole on the inside.
A plain seam up the heel
and the small piece X
sewed in for a tongue,
completes the sewing, and
the moccasin may be
turned right side out. It
should be gathered slightly in stitching the sole
and upper together
around the toe; these
gathers disappear on
dampening and stretching.

SIOUX OR PLAINS MOC-
CASIN PATTERN

Both these patterns of moccasins are fastened by leather thongs run through a series of
slits at the ankle. The Indian made article was
frequently decorated on the vamps with beads,

shells and colored porcupine quills. Sometimes the entire upper except around the ankle was a solid mass of bead designs. In some cases a piece of cloth was sewn to the leather to furnish a ground for beadwork. Bright embroidery silks look very nice on well dressed skins, and are used on most of the fancy moccasins sold at stores.

While there would be but little money in making these things for actual use they are in demand as souvenirs and can, especially the smaller sizes, be made up out of scraps of no value for other purposes. Sometimes too, a hunter may kill a deer and wish to remember a number of friends with little presents after having the head and horns mounted. The feet may be set up in four ornamental novelties and the hide would furnish certainly four assorted pairs of moccasins.

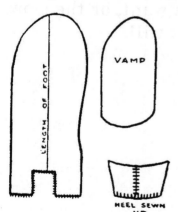

THE "WALLACE" MOC-
CASIN PATTERN

The moccasin pattern here shown is made and sold by A. F. Wallace, and it's a good one. It is not necessary to always have buckskin for mocks. Good ten or twelve oz. duck will wear well, and for night or bed slippers, the so called chamois skins of a sheep's back, do very well. No one can appreciate moccasins until they have worn them. If you rub your duck with paraffin wax, then iron it with a warm flatiron, it will be water proof, and the wear will surprise you. Of course buckskin is the proper thing, but sometimes it is in a buck's back, traveling through the timber.

If you are using mocks in snow, your wool socks will curl down over the top edge, forming the finest kind of a snow excluder. So don't worry about high moccasins, for snowshoeing or skiing.

When first wearing them, anything you step on will hurt your feet. If you sew an extra thickness on the bottom for a tap, letting it come well up on the sides, you will do away with this trouble. They are a good deal like "cracker jack," the more you eat, the more you want, or the more you wear mocks, the more you will.

CHAPTER XXXI.

UTILIZING FUR WASTE.

DURING the manufacture of furs there is necessarily much unavoidable waste in the form of small pieces, clippings and roundings as well as skins damaged and partially destroyed through improper treatment. All these are not allowed to become a total loss but are carefuly saved and sold to the dealers in fur cuttings after sorting into their several varieties.

Many of these scraps are bought by dealers in hatter's furs. The best hatter's fur is cut from the whole skin, is plucked to remove the guard hairs and chemically treated to facilitate felting. The hatter's fur obtained from fur cutter's waste is known as blown fur. The cuttings are run through a chopping machine and cut into small pieces and afterwards blown to separate the fur from the overhairs and pieces of skin. Blown fur is much shorter and less desirable than that cut or clipped from the skins.

Muskrat, fur seal, otter, beaver and mink are all used in this way. Some years ago the prices for cuttings ran about as follows:

Mink, Fur Seal ....15c per lb.
Muskrat ....35c to 40c per lb.
Otter ....45c per lb.
Beaver ....$1.00 to $1.25 per lb.

Many pieces and cuttings are used in other ways. Scraps of fur seal and muskrat are pieced together, dyed a uniform shade and made up in cheap furs. These are genuine furs but the many seams and the application of dye to the threads after sewing makes them very short-lived. I have seen a large robe composed entirely of muskrat clippings, set together with light and dark fur alternating. This was in the natural undyed state.

A mink robe, said by the owner to be fifty years old was brought in for repairs. The thread was giving way and the fur was considerably faded, but otherwise its condition was good, though made of scraps.

Such trimmings are sometimes made into linings where an even color is not necessary, warmth being the chief requisite. Small fur heads used in trimming are chiefly made from scraps, as are the fur covered buttons. Brush makers use parts of some skins in the production of artist's pencils.

CHAPTER XXXII.

CLEANING, REPAIRING AND STORING FURS.

THIS branch of the fur business, while not cutting much of a figure, will frequently prove the source of a small but steady income. As long as furs continue to be worn they will require to be cleaned and repaired, and people are coming more and more accustomed to having their furs stored and cared for during the warmer months of the year.

Professional cleaners claim that fur cleaning is one of the most risky branches of their business, as such articles cannot be treated like ordinary textile fabrics, and are often of great value. Nearly all furs (that is, manufactured skins), should be chemically cleaned, though in some cases soap and water can be employed to advantage.

In chemical cleaning or washing in gasoline, such cleaning is based upon the solvent power for grease which it possesses. Most discolorations of garments, both textile and fur, consist of dirt held by grease of various kinds collected during the wearing. By removing the grease the dirt is released and the stains disappear.

Gasoline vaporizes at ordinary temperatures, and such vapor is not absorbed by the atmosphere but seeks the floor level, where it will flow in the directions of any air currents which may be present. If this stream of vapor should come in contact with a flame in another room even, it would produce an immediate explosion and carry the fire back to the bulk of the cleaner being used. This mixture of gasoline, vapor and air is what, by ignition in the cylinders of the automobile engine, furnishes such dynamic power. Cleaning with gasoline in the ordinary dwelling is a dangerous proceeding and should be conducted with care anywhere.

So called spontaneous firing sometimes occurs, due to the generation of electric sparks. The rubbing or moving quickly of various materials in this volatile liquid may produce electric sparks, especially in frosty weather and when the air is dry. The addition of benzine soap in small quantities tends to prevent such sparking, and it also aids in the cleaning process.

All furs to be cleaned should be examined to ascertain if they are torn or ripped, or if any matches have gotten into them. Large, coarse skins used as rugs should have the heavy linings ripped out before cleaning, as they will soak up and waste much expensive material otherwise. Such skins like bear, tiger, leopard, sheep, goat

TWENTY-TWO RAW SILVER FOX SKINS VALUE THOUS-
ANDS OF DOLLARS

and dog, after being freed of lining are to be washed in gasoline, wrung out, rinsed in clean, wrung out and drummed with sawdust or meal until the fur is dry. Then hang in the open air or sun if possible to evaporate the fumes, beat well and after replacing the linings, comb out. If the rug has a full mounted head it, the head, should not be immersed in gasoline but cleaned with a brush. All furs should be absolutely dry and freed from all dust by thoroughly beating before cleaning.

In cleaning white furs especially, benzine soap is useful, though if it cannot be procured ready made from chemical dealers it may be dispensed with, as it is hardly worth while to make it unless a considerable work of this character is contemplated.

A solid benzine soap is made by putting about 8⅓ lbs. of white olein in an enameled kettle and while stirring pour in gradually one pound of 25% ammonia. Stir for three-fourths of an hour until it becomes hard. To use mix a small amount into paste with benzine and brush on the object to be cleaned. A little is added to the washing gasoline also.

White furs, muffs, collarettes, etc., are washed without removing the linings either with or without soap, brushed and rinsed twice, wringing after each rinse. Then work or drum in warm starch powder, potato or farina flour or talcum powder. Powdered gypsum leaves a gritty feeling in the fur and should not be used on fine furs. After cleaned furs are quite dry they should be entirely freed from any cleaning powder by beating, brushing and combing before wrapping up. Of course curly furs like angora and astrachan should never be combed.

In regard to repairing furs it may be truthfully said that "a stitch in time saves nine," and nothing spoils the appearance of a fine piece of fur more than a neglected rip or tear. Be sure and give all work of this class thorough inspection, as furs are often in a condition which the owner does not suspect. What appears to be whole skins may in reality be composed of small pieces, or many rips and tears be hidden by a heavy pelage.

All skin sewing should be done from the back, so the ripping and resewing of linings should be calculated on. To repair garments by replacing worn parts with new skins is difficult to do properly. Sometimes it becomes necessary to cut it down, that is, shorten a coat or shorten or narrow a collarette slightly, and use the best of what is trimmed off to repair worn places. Rugs and laprobes that are in use require to have their linings and borders renewed occasionally to prolong their usefulness. Collarette chains, hooks and muff guards are lost, broken and altogether minor repairs aggregate quite an item. Collars and cuffs of new fur will go far toward freshening up an old coat.

For storing quantities of furs, cold storage space is best, but an ordinary room may be made use of, if it is dry, cool and not too light. All furs received for storage should have tags written in ink sealed on in the owner's presence, and have a valuation set on them at the same time so they may be insured. The condition, any damage or need of repair should be noted on the storage tags. Beat the furs out well before hanging away.

The chief insect enemy of garment furs is the larva of several species of moths. The mature winged specimens do no damage, but from their eggs are hatched the tiny white worms which delight in shaving the fur from skins, both raw and dressed. The dermestes or "bacon beetle" chiefly attacks raw skins and hides but the moth is more impartial, browsing alike on carpets, hangings, cloth and fur garments.

Such things cannot have their entire surface poisoned as the taxidermist treats mounted specimens, on account of the danger to those wearing or handling them. The moth larva is most destructive in the warm months, from May to October, but in heated rooms the work may continue through the winter months. They are killed by immersion in benzine or exposure to the fumes of carbon bisulphide.

The ordinary wall showcases for garments answer very well for storing a few furs, and additional cases of the same shape may be made of tongue and grooved boards with close fitting wooden, instead of glass doors. Hang all furs in these cases on suitable hangers and leave exposed in the bottom of the cases a quantity of naphthaline crystals or pure gum camphor, either of which disseminate fumes distasteful to the moth family. If the glass front cases are used cover the furs with muslin, as a strong continuous light tends to fade most dark furs.

If an entire room is used, equip it with poles like curtain poles on which to hook hangers. Keep it dark and carry an electric torch when visiting it. Make it a rule to require two or three days' notice, when furs are withdrawn from storage, as they should be beaten, combed and well aired before returning.

CHAPTER XXXIII.

PRICES FOR TANNING AND OTHER FUR WORK.

THERE is naturally considerable range in the charges for work of this nature, dependent on the condition of the material, etc. This is not always so apparent to the general public as to the skin expert, and often the best that can be done is to strike an average that will let the good jobs make up for the unprofitable ones. There is, too, always the satisfaction of work well done. To the beginner especially, the usual charges for skin dressing seem trivial compared to the amount of labor expended. With practice the work can be finished off much more rapidly and the local workman can nearly always get an advance on the rates of a professional at a distance. A customer is nearly always willing to pay the regular rates plus the express charges to the nearest large establishment; if the work is what it should be.

The annexed list gives the usual range of charges, the lowest figure being for the small skins of the kind and in good condition and the highest for those not so well handled or the very largest in size.

BEATING BEAVER SKINS FOR REMOVING SAWDUST, ETC.

TANNING PRICES

Badger ....$0.50 to $0.75
Beaver .... .75 to 1.00
Bears—
    Black .... 1.00 to 4.00
    Polar .... 4.00 to 12.00
    Grizzly .... 2.00 to 6.00
Cats-—
    House .... .25

Cats—Continued

Wild	$0.50	to	$1.00
Ringtail	.25		
Cow	5.00	to	8.00
Calf	1.00	to	3.00
Deer	1.00	to	2.50
Fawn	.50	to	1.00
Dogs	.50	to	3.00
Elk	3.00	to	5.00
Fisher	.15	to	1.00

Foxes—

Gray	.50	to	75
Red	.50	to	75
Kit	.25	to	50
White	.75	to	1.00
Silver	1.00	to	1.50

Goats—

Common	1.00	to	2.00
Angora	1.50	to	2.50
Hare	.15		
Horse	5.00	to	8.00
Jaguar	1.00	to	3.00
Leopard	1.00	to	2.50
Lion	3.00	to	6.00
Lynx	.75	to	1.00
Marten	.25	to	50
Mink	.25	to	50
Moose	3.00	to	6.00
Mole	.10		

Muskrat	$0.10 to	$0.25
Opossum	.10 to	25
Otter	.75 to	1.00
Puma	1.00 to	3.00
Rabbit	.10 to	15
Raccoon	.35 to	75
Seal—		
Hair	1.00	
Wool	1.00	
Sheep	1.00 to	2.50
Lambs	.50 to	1.50
Skunk	.35 to	50
Civet Skunk	.25	
Squirrels	.25	
Tiger	3.00 to	8.00
Weasels	.10	
Wolves—		
Timber	1.00 to	1.25
Coyotes	.75 to	1.00
Wolverine	1.00	
Woodchuck	.25	

TANNING LEATHER.

Cow and Horse, for glove leather	5.00 to	8.00
Deer, Sheep, Goat, for buckskin.	1.00 to	1.50
Alligator—		
To 3 ft. in length..........	1.00	
3 to 4 ft. in length........	1.50 to	2.00
4 to 5 ft. in length........	2.00 to	3.00

Alligator—Continued

    5 to 7 ft. in length.........$3.00 to $5.00

Snake—

    Under 4 ft................   50 to   1.00

    4 to 7 ft................. 1.25 to   2.50

    Over 7 ft................ 3.00 to 10.00

DYEING (BLACK OR BROWN)

Cattle and Horse.............	2.50		
Goat	.75	to	2.50
Coyote	1.00		
Mink	.35		
Marten	.35		
Fox	1.00		
Muskrat.......................	.25		
Sheep	.75	to	1.50
Dog	.75	to	1.50
Calf	.75	to	1.50
Wolf	1.50		
Skunk	.50		
Opossum	.35		
Lynx	1.50		
Raccoon	.50	to	.75
Wild Cat	1.00		
House Cat	.50		

MISCELLANEOUS

Fur Purses, small	.25	to	50
Fur Hand Bags, small.........	75	to	1.50

MISCELLANEOUS—CONTINUED

Snake Hand Bags ....$1.00 to $2.50
Snake Purses or Matchholders..   50 to   1.00
Buckskin, Calf or Fawn Vests... 4.00
Moccasins, plain, per pair...... 1.00
Snake Belts 2.50
Snake Hat Bands 1.00
Plain Mittens from horse, cow,
    calf or dog skins, per pair.. 1.00
Gauntlet Mittens from same.   1.50
Leather Mittens   50
Gauntlet Mittens, coon or musk-
    rat 3.50
Gauntlet Gloves, coon or muskrat 4.50
Gauntlet Gloves from horse, cow,
    calf or dog skins........... 2.25
Fur Caps, according to material,
    from horse, or cow hide to
    muskrat at $4.00 and mink.. 6.00
Ladies' Auto Hoods and Soft
    Hats, according to material. 5.00 to 12.00
Fur Collars .... 2.50 to 3.50

FUR COATS.

On these the charges will run from say $8.00
on a man's coat of cow hide to $200.00 for a lady's
long mink coat. Ladies' short coats in the
coarser furs are made up for $12.00 to $15.00 each
which is about what is charged for men's in rac-

coon or wild cat furs. At these figures the linings,etc., are furnished, but the cost of tanning must be added.

﹂aking fur lined coats costs from \$20.00 to \$40.00 each in coarse hides, like cow or horse, and \$100.00 to \$150.00 in skins like mink, according to the grade of material used in the cover. These figures are in addition to the tanning.

In the matter of muffs and neckpieces there is the greatest variation, owing to the different patterns and the varying number of skins required. With the dressing charges included, muffs cost ﹐rom \$2.50 to \$3.00 for children's to \$5.00, \$i0.00 and even \$25.00 for ladv's sizes. The extreme prices are of course for work requiring a number of fine skins like mink ﹐r marten.

On neckpieces the range is as great, fr﹐m the plain lined neck band made from one small skin for \$2.00 to the mink or marten shawl of a dozen skins or over, for the construction of which \$35.00 will hardly pay. Sets of fox or raccoon in common shapes usually cost about \$15.00 for making both neckpiece and muff.

FUR ROBES.

This is an article the cost of making can be closely estimated, any variation being due to extra size or quality of linings. They are ordinarily made with a single felt border and black or green plush lining, and these prices are based on such material, not including the tanning charges.

Horse or Cow Skin.............$5.00
Calf, Dog, Goat or Sheep.   5.00 to $6.00
Fox, Coon, Wild Cat........... 9.00 to 10.00
Wolf, Coyote 8.50
Muskrat ....15.00 to 20.00

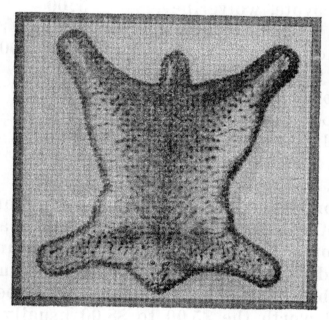

WILD CAT RUG, OPEN MOUTH

ANIMAL FUR RUGS.

The prices given are for lining all rugs not larger than a fox with all felt and trimming with a double border of same. Large skins to have the double felt border but lined with art denim or canvas.

Rugs wanted with open mouths must have the natural teeth with them, or an extra charge must be made.

NAME	CLOSED MOUTH	OPEN MOUTH
Fox, raccoon, badger, wild cat, house cat	$4.50	$5.50
Lynx, coyote, wolverine.	5.00	6.00
Timber wolf	6.00	7.00
Dogs, according to size..	4.00-10.00	5.00-15.00
Puma, jaguar, leopard..	10.00	12.00
Bear, brown or black ..	12.00	15.00
Bear, polar or grizzly...	16.00	20.00
Tiger, lion	20.00	25.00
Deer	10.00	
Goat	8.00	

For cleaning furs, such as a muff or neck-piece of white fox, the charge is $1.00 for a single piece or $1.50 for the set. Other cleaning is charged for according to the amount of material and labor necessary. To clean a polar bear rug is well worth the $5.00 to $8.00 usually asked. Storage charges depend considerably on the value of the furs charged, and are so much per month, with a minimum charge of 25 or 50 cents.

Repairs and orders for new work sent in during the dull season are usually figured at a much lower rate than when left until the last moment, before they are wanted.

CHAPTER XXXIV

APPENDIX.

THE variety of tools and materials men-tioned as being useful or indispensable to the home manufacturer of furs makes a list that is bewildering to the beginner perhaps. Well all of them are not needed at once, fortun-ately.

"Where can I get them?" some one says. There are dealers in furrier's supplies who handle nearly all except the chemical supplies for fur dressing, but many of the necessaries are to be had near home as readily if we look for them in the right place. The grocery store will furnish soaps, lye or potash, borax, salt and often quite a list of other things, depending on the proprie-tor's ideas of what a grocery should be. Water is to be had most anywhere, but not always the best water for the purpose. On the subject of water, soap, etc., a practical man says:

"Two very important things, and I might say the most important of all, are the soap and water used in the processes here mentioned. If you wish to make a good job, the *water must be soft,* i. e., 'either rain or soft river water.' Be sure spring water is soft if you use it. Rain water is best of all. A simple test for the hardness of the water is soap, the common cheap bar kind. Take a piece and a dish of cold water wash your hands in it, using plenty of the above soap; if it curdles, it is unfit for use in tanning (or anything else) although it can be used for drinking and cooking purposes. Neither in such water can you cure meat for smoking

As before mentioned, the soap comes next in importance, and the best of all is the old-fashioned soft soap, made by the old-time farmers, by setting up a barrel or leach with a little coarse straw in the bottom through which a half dozen one inch holes have been bored. Then fill with good hardwood ashes, set up on a tight bench eighteen inches high, in which a groove has been cut about one-half inch deep, around the bottom of the barrel where it rests on the platform, and leaking into the spot where you wish to catch the leakings from the barrel. Soft water poured into the top

BARREL OR ASH LEACH

of the barrel, into a pan shaped hole in the ashes, will in a few hours produce the best kind of lye for your soap.

Take a twelve quart pail full of lye, bring to a boil and add grease enough in the shape of ham or bacon rinds, bones and any old grease (animal not mineral) until the mixture is the consistency of jelly when cold. More soap can be made by using more of the material in proportion; if too thin bring up to a boil, and add more grease, and if too thick add more lye; let it boil two hours, stirring constantly, before taking sample to cool.

This is the best soap ever except for wounds. Assuming you haven't a leach or ashes for making the lye, then use the following: To ten pounds of grease take eight and a half pounds of pure white potash, (buy the latter in fine lumps) place the potash in the bottom of a good strong water-tight barrel, boil the grease and pour it *boiling hot* on the potash, then add one pail of boiling water and stir all together. The next morning, add one pail cold water and stir one-half hour. Continue this until the barrel contains eighteen gallons. Let stand one week and it is ready for use. The potash can be added to the grease or vice versa, but each must be done while boiling. By adding another one-half pound resin, you have the old-fashioned soap, and it can be run into cakes. But for tanning, leave the resin out.

While we are around bothering the grocer, we might as well get some wooden lard tubs and a vinegar barrel or so for tan vats, and if he has some empty boxes a few of them will be useful to make fur stretchers, cleaning drums and trays of. Corn meal and bran for cleaning and tanning come from the feed store and gasoline from grocery, paint store or garage. Quite an assortment of tools may be selected at almost any hardware dealers, though it is not likely that special tanners' and dressers' tools can be had there.

Some of the useful chemicals such as sulphate of iron, sulphate of copper, sulphate, bicarbonate and hyposulphate of soda, are to be had of dealers in agricultural or veterinary supplies. In procuring chemicals for tanning at a drug house it is well to remember that what is known as the commercial quality is as suitable for such use as the C. P. or chemically pure, and usually much cheaper. Alcohol, lime, calcined or plaster of Paris, sandpaper and a number of other things can be bought with the most economy of the paint dealer.

Modeling clay is furnished by dealers in artist's materials, but the blue or white clay from a pottery is just as good, or you may get it from

the bank yourself if it is convenient. That prepared for use has been freed from lumps and grit.

Any enterprising dry goods house will provide a fair assortment of lining material, thread,
etc., and patterns for muffs, collarettes, caps,
etc., may be bought there or ordered by mail from
the pattern companies. Of course the goods most
suitable or the easiest to use may not be in
stock, but probably some suitable substitute will
be at hand which may possibly answer as well or
better. Colored felts are handled by dealers in
upholstery, as are the art denims. Heavy coating material is often substituted for plush as
robe lining, and the overall variety of denim
cannot be beat for wear as lining for large rugs.
Of late years it has been possible to procure ready
to use muff beds from some of the large dry goods
houses, as they are in demand for use in making
muffs of some of the new "fur cloths." These
cloths, such as "astrachan," "pony skin" and
others, make beautiful robe linings.

A few items are never found in stock except
at dealers in taxidermists' and furriers' supplies,
such as skin worker's tools, fur knives and combs,
muff blocks, artificial head forms, glass eyes and
special fur dyes. In the United States, New
York City and Montreal in British America are
the headquarters for dealers in furriers' supplies.

MINK TRAPPING

introduction says: V
many excellent mir
one man has studied out
ods, for the conditions
the trapper in the Sou
largest catches would p
little value to the trapp
North, where snow cove
the greater part of the y

Conditions along the A
ferent than the Pacific,
methods used by thousan
along the Mississippi and
differ from the Eastern or
trapper, for the mink's :
same along the fresh in
the coast or salt water.

The methods explaine
are from all parts of t
many experienced trappe
best methods, so that it makes no difference in
America you live, valuable information on best tr
for your locality, will no doubt, be found.

Mink Trapping contains nearly 171 pages, about
and nineteen chapters as follows:

Ginseng and Other Medicinal Plants

A Valuable Book for Growers and Collectors of Wild Medicinal Plants—Tells How to Grow, Medicinal Uses, Etc.

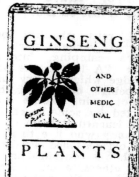

THIS book, Revised Edition, contains 367 pages and about 100 illustrations, 40 being Ginseng, showing this plant in various stages of development, both cultivated and wild; also roots of different sizes and quality with explanation of value, etc. There are 20 illustrations of Golden Seal, showing plants and roots at different stages of growth. With about 160 pages are devoted to Ginseng and more than 50 to Golden Seal—all of interest to growers, diggers and sellers.

Some 40 other roots, plants and herbs having medicinal value are shown and briefly described.

The raising of GINSENG and GOLDEN SEAL (the wild supply of which is nearly gone) are proving profitable.

This book contains Thirty-five chapters as follows:

Among the Plants described in Chapters XXVII to XXXV and which furnish Root Drugs are: Male Fern; Wild Turnip; Skunk Cabbage; Sweet Flag; Helonias; American Hellebore; Aletris; Bethroot; Wild Yam; Serpentaria (Southern Snakeroot); Yellow Dock; Soapwort; Goldthread; Oregon Grape; Twinleaf; Canada Moonseed; Bloodroot; Hydrangea; Indian Physic; Wild Indigo; Crane's Bill; Stilling; Wild Sarsaparilla; Water Frynged; American Angelica, Yellow Jasmine; Pinkroot; American Colomba; Black Indian Hemp; Pleurisy Root; Comfrey; Stoneroot; Culinarys Root; Dandelion; Queen-of-the-Meadow; Elecampane; Echimena; Burdock. A good photograph of each is shown with the description. Considerable money can be made collecting and preparing wild roots for the market. This book will give you the needed "know-how."

Price, postpaid, paper bound, $2.00

A. R. HARDING PUB. CO.

2878 E. Main St.   Columbus, Ohio 43209

Camp and Trail Methods

*Interesting Information for All Lovers of Nature—
the Outdoors. What to Take and What to Do.*

THE author, E. Kreps, who has spent several years in various parts of North America camping, hunting, and trapping, says: "A life in the open air calls for knowledge which a very large number of human beings, because of their environments, cannot gain, except when the same is imparted by some more fortunate one who has learned it from experience. There are many who live this outdoor life and these old seasoned woodsmen know, perhaps, all that is contained in this book, but there are others, a much larger number, who do not know the many things relating to outdoor life, which it is almost necessary that one should be well ecquainted with when he or she make their first trip into the fastnesses of Mother Nature.

"There are many books on woodcraft, written by sportsmen, fishermen, and campers, but only a few of these books were written by practical woodsmen and for people who want to belong to that class. Such books are intended for the big game hunter, or the fisherman who goes for a short stay into some easily accessible location, well equipped and with a guide who does all the work and looks after the comfort of those whom he has in charge. This book is a decided departure from that class, as it not only gives the information needed by the tourist and summer camper, but gives special attention to the needs of those practical ones whose calling, whatever it may be, leads them into the wilds and holds them there at all times of the year; the hunter, the fisherman, the trapper, the prospector, the surveyor; all these and many ohers will find much valuable information in this book"

This practical books contains 274 pages and 68 illustrations. There are 19 chapters as follows:

As the author says, this book is so written that it is of value to anyone who camps or goes upon the "trail." Read the chapter headings carefully. This book tells *what to take* and *what* to *do*. The book is attractively bound in cloth, printed on good paper, size 5x7 inches.

Price, postpaid, paper bound, $1.50

A. R. HARDING, Pub., 2878 E. Main St., Columbus, O. 43209